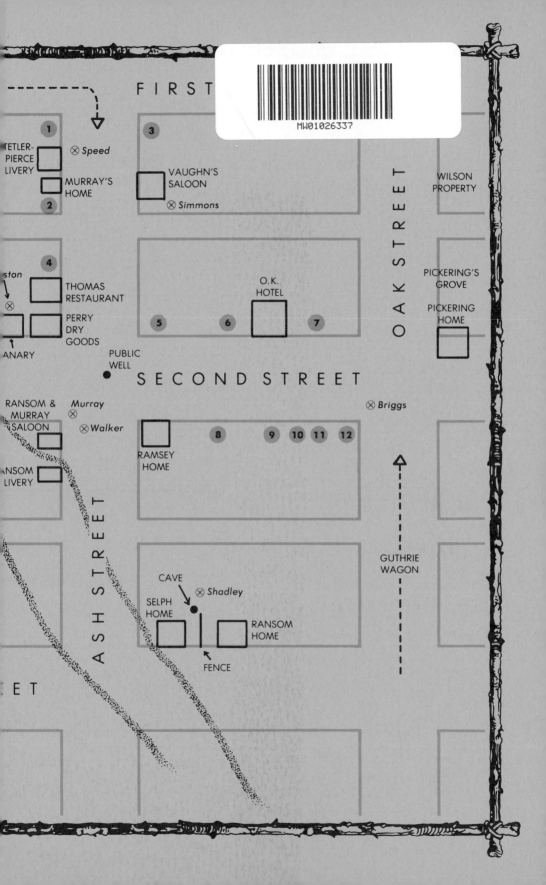

FIRST

① 1

TETLER-
PIERCE
LIVERY   ⊗ *Speed*

                MURRAY'S
                HOME
② 2

③ 3
                VAUGHN'S
                SALOON
                ⊗ *Simmons*

ston
④ 4
                THOMAS
                RESTAURANT

⊗
                PERRY
                DRY
                GOODS
ANARY

⑤ 5   ⑥ 6   O.K.
                        HOTEL   ⑦ 7

        PUBLIC
        WELL
        ●   SECOND STREET

RANSOM &   *Murray*   ⊗ *Briggs*
MURRAY   ⊗
SALOON   ⊗ *Walker*

                                ⑧ 8   ⑨ 9 ⑩ 10 ⑪ 11 ⑫ 12
NSOM
LIVERY
                RAMSEY
                HOME

                                        GUTHRIE
                                        WAGON

            CAVE   ⊗ *Shadley*
            SELPH   ●
            HOME
                        RANSOM
                        HOME

                FENCE

OAK STREET

ASH STREET

WILSON
PROPERTY

PICKERING'S
GROVE

PICKERING
HOME

GUNFIGHT AT INGALLS
DEATH OF AN OUTLAW TOWN

GUNFIGHT AT INGALLS

DEATH OF AN OUTLAW TOWN

GLENN SHIRLEY

Barbed Wire Press

Stillwater, Oklahoma

Library of Congress Cataloging-in-Publication Data

Shirley, Glenn.
    Gunfight at Ingalls: death of an outlaw town/Glenn Shirley.—1st ed.
        p.   cm.
    Includes bibliographical references and index.
    ISBN 0-935269-06-1
    1. Ingalls (Okla.)—History. 2. Frontier and pioneer life—Oklahoma—Ingalls.
3. Outlaws—Oklahoma—Ingalls—History—19th century. 4. Violence—Oklahoma—Ingalls—History—19th century.
I. Title.
F704.I54S55   1990   90-885
976.6'34—dc20   CIP

Cover and book design by L.A. Smith

Copyright © 1990 by Glenn Shirley
All rights reserved
Published by Barbed Wire Press, P.O. Box 2107, Stillwater, OK 74076
Manufactured in the United States of America

CONTENTS

MAPS AND
ILLUSTRATIONS

PREFACE

AT INGALLS, OKLAHOMA Territory, on the early autumn morning of September 1, 1893, a posse of thirteen deputy United States marshals sought to break up and capture the notorious Bill Doolin band of outlaws, who were making this isolated though promising frontier village a pop-off valve and refuge between their numerous bank and train robberies. In the exchange of gunfire, three officers and two bystanders were slain; one gang member and two citizen-participants were seriously wounded; and one outlaw was captured. The deadly battle climaxed the bringing of law and order to Oklahoma and Indian territories.

Ingalls, as a town, has vanished. Only an imported log cabin, a run-down Odd Fellows hall used for storage, a frame community building once used as a schoolhouse, and a vandalized native stone memorial to the fallen marshals now mark the vicinity of the gunfight. Even the signs put up by local citizens pointing out sites of the other buildings and the places where men died have been carried away or are too faded for the visitor to read the messages they once bore.

Efforts toward historic preservation of the battle site made down the years have failed for various reasons. For over half a century I have collected eyewitness accounts and contemporary and official reports of what transpired at Ingalls before and after that fatal day in 1893. I have briefed these in previous outlaw-lawman biographies, and included them as chapters in a couple of volumes. But chapters, many of my readers declare, are too insignificant in describing this important occurrence on our bygone frontier. They insist, "You ought to write a book."

Gunfight at Ingalls: Death of an Outlaw Town is that book.

GLENN SHIRLEY

Stillwater, Oklahoma
March 1990

GUNFIGHT AT INGALLS
DEATH OF AN OUTLAW TOWN

THE STAGE
AND THE SETTING
1

INGALLS WOULD NOT have suffered the ignominy of
the bloodiest gunfight between organized banditry and
peace officers in the history of the West, and might not
have died, but for the amnesty and friendship it extended
the "king" of Oklahoma Territory outlaws, Bill Doolin,
and his so-called "Wild Bunch."

The little town lay ten miles east of Stillwater and five
miles north of the Cimarron River, between the Little
Stillwater and Council Creek tributaries, and three miles
inside the then eastern boundary of Payne County—one
of six counties carved from the Unassigned Lands opened
in Oklahoma's first race for homes on April 22, 1889.
Isolated in this remote corner of the new territory, far from
a railroad and off main traveled trails, there seemed to be
no reason for its birth.

North of the Payne County line, in the Cherokee Outlet,
the Berry Brothers of Sumner County, Kansas, ran 4,000
head of cattle, mules, and horses on some 19,000 acres
leased from the Cherokee Strip Livestock Association.
Before they had to abandon this southern portion of their
grazing area to homestead settlement, they dreamed of a
60,000-acre kingdom extending to the Cimarron. Northeast
of Payne County, on the Pawnee Indian reservation and
in the "Triangle" or "Flat Iron" country formed by the

1

confluence of the Cimarron and Arkansas rivers, association members Ed Hewins and Milt Bennett pastured 10,000
head of Texas and Mexico cattle on their 105,456-acre
Bar X Bar range. South of the Pawnees, on the Sac and Fox
reservation between the Cimarron and Deep Fork rivers,
the Saginaw Cattle Company of Saginaw, Michigan,
operated a vast ranching enterprise known as the Turkey
Track. East of the Pawnee and Sac and Fox reservations
lay the Creek Nation of the Five Civilized Tribes.

Almost every tract of 160 acres in eastern Payne County
had been occupied. A town was needed by the area's rural
population. A few miles through mud and over unmarked
trails was far enough to go for mail, supplies, and patent
medicines. In June 1889, two enterprising homesteaders,
Dr. Robert F. McMurtry and Robert Beal, each released forty
acres from their original quarter-sections to be used as a
townsite and named it for United States Senator John James
Ingalls of Kansas, who had been instrumental in getting
the Unassigned Lands opened to settlement.

More than a score of similar small towns sprang up in
Payne County in its earliest history. Most of them have
disappeared and are virtually forgotten. A few remembered
in the eastern half of the county, besides Ingalls, are Ransom, Windom, Payne Center, Otego, and Clayton. Every
town had a general store, which usually doubled as a post
office; some had drugstores, schools, churches, and all
were centers of community life for years before they were
eliminated by progress and improved roads and bridges
to larger towns.

Ingalls had a distinct advantage. One Stillwater
newspaper observed, "The townsite is well located and
will admit to the building of a beautiful town. The slope
is just enough for drainage, which is so essential to good
health. It is surrounded by rolling prairie that has...as
much bottom land as any other point in Oklahoma. This
land will produce from 50 to 75 bushels of corn per acre.
The proximity of the Little Stillwater, Council Creek and
Cimarron River insure well-watered soil that will make
almost any crop thrive.... Trade from the Indian reservations contingent to Ingalls is a desirable one and will con-

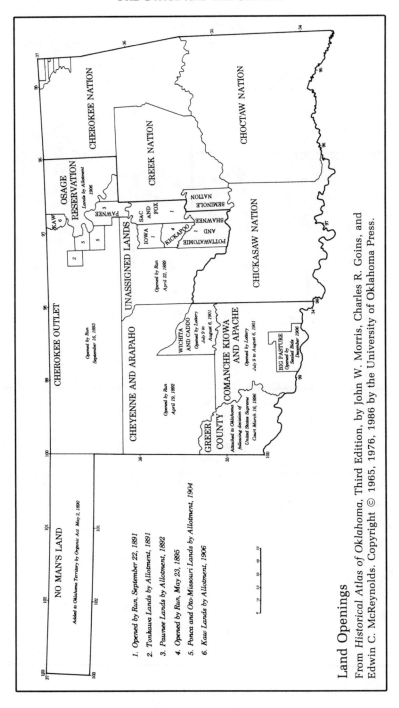

Land Openings

From *Historical Atlas of Oklahoma*, Third Edition, by John W. Morris, Charles R. Goins, and Edwin C. McReynolds. Copyright © 1965, 1976, 1986 by the University of Oklahoma Press.

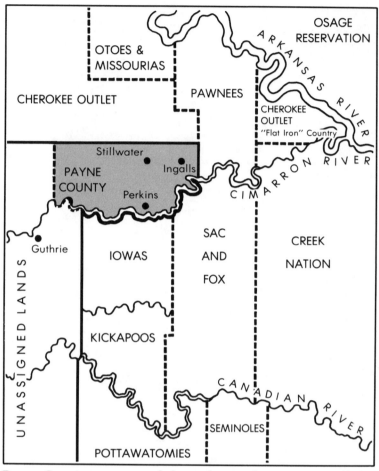

Payne County was carved from the northeast corner of the
Unassigned Lands.

tribute materially to the prosperity of the city.''

Ingalls faced competition of a sort. About three miles southeast of the site, near the Pawnee reservation border, a trading post with a store and mail drop had served the Indians and cowboys before the opening. Less than a mile west was a big spring where water making its way to the Cimarron flowed over the top of a rock that formed a cave. The waterfall had suggested the name of the post—Falls City.

Joseph D. Vickrey of Bolivar, Missouri, had taken the claim on which Falls City was located. He brought his wife and four children here, built a home, and set up a blacksmith shop. Across the road, which was the township line, Sherman "Sherm" Sanders, a former Turkey Track cowboy, constructed a log house and opened a barber shop. Sanders did not get a claim in the run of eighty-nine, but soon afterwards had obtained a relinquishment from a man named Pound.

Since the opening, settlers for miles around had picked up their mail and supplies at Falls City. Beal and McMurtry, however, were not deterred. Their eighty acres were surveyed into a square town of sixteen blocks, and the eastern half platted. It consisted of nine full and seven fraction blocks, with four north-south streets named Main, Walnut, Ash, and Oak, and four east-west avenues numbered First (also called Section Line Road), Second, Third, and Fourth. Main Street was on the west side of the townsite. Streets were 100 feet wide, alleys 20 feet.

On Second, at Oak Street, McMurtry constructed a small frame building for an undertaking parlor and a drugstore. In November, he was elected community coroner. On the north side of First (the main trail into Ingalls east and west) and opposite the center of the townsite, Beal opened a general store and corral. Beal bought and sold horses, harness, and saddles. He kept his horses in a pasture on the A.B. Querry homestead a couple of miles south on the Main Street road.

McMurtry obtained a grant for a post office, which he set up in the corner of his drugstore. He was appointed the town's first postmaster on January 22, 1890, and

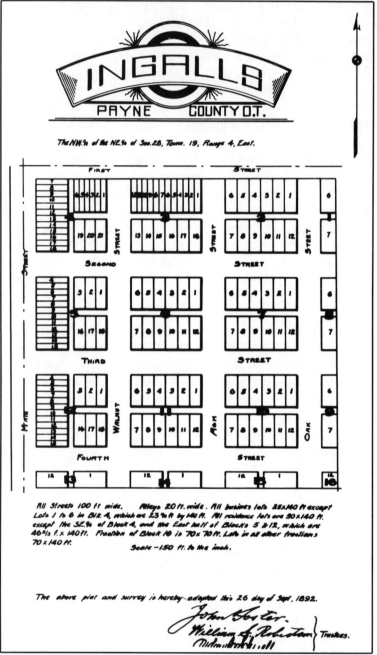

Original plat of Ingalls, O.T., adopted September 26, 1892.

thereafter, the people got their mail by hack and rider from Stillwater.

McMurtry filled the office only a few months. Declining health forced him to resign. He relinquished the position to J.W. Ellsworth, a notary public and part-time minister who had come to Ingalls with his wife and daughter, Edith, from Iowa via Missouri. Dr. McMurtry died shortly afterward, and his widow turned the drugstore into a notions shop. Another physician, W.R. Call, who "made a specialty of compounding recipes with accuracy and dispatch," opened a pharmacy on Second, west of McMurtry's.

Meanwhile, embryo Oklahoma grew rapidly. On May 2, 1890, President Benjamin Harrison signed into law the congressional act which created the six counties from the Unassigned Lands—Logan, Oklahoma, Cleveland, Canadian, Kingfisher, and Payne, with seat towns at Guthrie, Oklahoma City, Norman, El Reno, Kingfisher, and Stillwater, respectively. The act also extended the territory to include the following areas: the Public Land Strip (No Man's Land) as a seventh county called Beaver, with the seat at Beaver; all of former Indian Territory except the reservations proper of the Five Civilized Tribes; the seven small reservations of the Quapaw Agency northeast of the Cherokee Nation; the portion of the Cherokee Outlet not occupied by the Ponca, Tonkawa, Oto-Missouri, and Pawnee Indians; and the Greer country between the north and south forks of Red River (then in dispute with Texas) in the event that the Supreme Court adjudged the title thereto should be vested in the United States.

The government prescribed consisted of a governor as the chief executive, a secretary of the territory, a U.S. district attorney, and a U.S. marshal, all appointed by the president of the United States; a legislative assembly of thirteen council members and a twenty-six member house of representatives elected by the people; and a judicial system of district, probate, and justice of the peace courts, with a supreme court consisting of a chief justice and two associate justices. The territory was divided into three districts, with one of the three justices holding court in each of the districts, as well as serving as a member of the appellate court. Guthrie was designated the territorial capital until such time as the legislative assembly and the governor might establish it elsewhere.

President Harrison provided a full complement of officials. County boundaries were defined, county governments established, legislative districts marked off. The population was enumerated, and the first representatives were elected on August 5. The first legislative assembly, meeting at Guthrie on August 27, adopted a code of laws taken from the statute books of various states, mainly Nebraska.

The settlers did not enter the Unassigned Lands in time to seed their farms. That, coupled with a severe drought in 1890, left many of them destitute. Congress appropriated $47,000 for relief, and a territorial board of three was named to administer the program. Congress also had approved $50,000 for the temporary support of a common school system yet to be set up. On the higher education level, Edmond got a normal school, Norman a university, and Stillwater the agricultural and mechanical college. Finally, the legislature provided for farming out the territory's convicts to the Kansas state penitentiary at Lansing and its insane to Illinois.

Payne County's population increased to nearly 7,000, some 600 of whom lived in Stillwater. Stillwater boasted of 50 business and 158 residence buildings, about 60 frame structures used as barns, buggy sheds, and similar shelters, and 21 water wells. Ill feelings still smoldered over its designation as the county seat. The major contenders had been Payne Center, a village of 147 persons three miles to the south, and the town of Perkins, about ten miles southwest at the extreme edge of the county, on the bank of the Cimarron. The actions of supporters on all sides almost resulted in violence and gunplay before the controversy ended.

Payne Center ceased to exist. Its few buildings were dismantled; some were moved to Stillwater, but most became a source of lumber for Ingalls. Perkins survived, reasoning that it would be centrally located when more

Sherman "Sherm" Sanders and family in front of log home on his claim at Falls City, southeast of Ingalls, O.T.

Robert "Bob" Beal home north of Ingalls, O.T.

land was added to the county with the opening of the Indian reservations to the south. The town built a substan-
tial bridge across the Cimarron at its own expense to
prepare for that time and event.

Ingalls looked both south and north for its development.
Under provisions of the Dawes Act of 1887, as amended
in February of 1891, each member of an Indian tribe on
a reservation could be allotted eighty acres and the surplus
lands opened to settlement. Negotiations had been completed with the Cherokees in the spring of 1890 for relinquishment of the Outlet west of the ninety-sixth meridian,
and preparations were under way for its opening in 1893.
Plans already were afoot to attach five townships to Payne
County with that opening. Agreements made with the
Iowa, Sac and Fox, and the Pottawatomie and Absentee
Shawnee Indians in June were ratified by Congress on
February 13 and March 3, 1891, respectively. Cattle out-
fits with grazing leases, like the Turkey Track, were
removed. After 2,718 Indians received their allotments, ap-
proximately 900,000 acres remained in the reservations east
of the old Unassigned Lands district. That area was opened
in Oklahoma's second race for homes on September 22,
1891.

An estimated 20,000 home seekers participated. Except-
ing the sections reserved for schools, practically every acre
was occupied. Government surveyors had located two
towns—Chandler in the north and Tecumseh in the
south—and named their postmaster prior to the opening.
Those towns got the big play and became the seats of the
two counties formed—County "A" and County "B," later
named Lincoln and Pottawatomie. In addition, Logan,
Oklahoma, and Cleveland counties were enlarged to the
east, and Payne County gained that portion lying south of
the Cimarron.

Across the river southeast of Ingalls, on the old roundup grounds of the Turkey Track, William Rae "Billy" Little, a former cowboy in the Pawnee country and government trader at the Sac and Fox agency, founded a competitive town on eighty acres of his homestead. Named
Cushing, the town soon had a blacksmith shop, general

store, home and business shop, dry-goods store, a saloon, and drugstore. Several more business houses were under construction.

Ingalls still looked toward the Outlet and continued to grow. Bill Wilson, who had homesteaded east of the square on Section Line Road, put in a general store at First and Oak. North of Section Line Road and the Wilson place some acreage was obtained for a cemetery. On the west side of Ash, at First, where the wagon road entered the town from the west, Alonzo J. Light built a residence and blacksmith shop. South of Light's, on Ash, Henry Franklin "Hank" Pierce and William P. "Bill" Hostetter opened a livery and feed stable.

Then, unexpectedly, it looked as if Ingalls would be dissolved.

In the spring of 1892, a man named J. Shaftsbury living just west of Ingalls filed a contest on the unplatted forty acres, claiming abandonment. A town meeting was held and Doctor Call and Bill Hostetter were sent to Guthrie to investigate. They employed an attorney for fifty dollars and were advised they possibly could beat the contest but that it would be cheaper to compromise with Shaftsbury.

There were other flies in the ointment. Delegations from six nearby points hurried to the territorial capital to present arguments that the trading center be placed elsewhere. Ingalls sent another delegation, headed by Arch Witt, a homesteader from north of town.

Witt and others solicited donations until another fifty dollars for an attorney was subscribed. They waited until the meeting with the U.S. land commission was in full swing, then "marched in and showed why Ingalls should be saved." The commission was satisfied with the report of the town's progress. That displeased the representatives from the other places, and the meeting broke up in a row.

Shaftsbury got the west forty acres, but Ingalls stayed. On September 26, 1892, the survey and plat of the east forty acres (NW¼ of the NE¼ of Section 28, Township 19, Range 4 East of the Indian meridian) was approved by townsite trustees John Foster, William Robertson, and Andrew C. Schenell, all of Guthrie, appointed by the secretary of the interior and known as Townsite Board No. 6.

The town lots were deeded by the U.S. commissioners in October. The trustees listed in a book the location and value of each lot, then held hearings to determine the right of all claimants. Priority was given those already occupying the townsite, evidenced by improvements. The Ingalls tract book, filed with the Register of Deeds in Payne County, lists the purchasers and lots, which were valued at two to four dollars each.

Rumors flew that the railroad was coming through that portion of Payne County and that the town was destined to become a metropolis. People from all the places that had pressed for the trading point began rushing to Ingalls to obtain the best locations.

Sherm Sanders, deciding to get a piece of the action, moved his barber business from Falls City to a shop south of the Pierce-Hostetter livery and feed barn. A block south of Light's blacksmith shop, on Ash at Second, John Wesley "Preacher" Perry opened a dry-goods store.

Perry was a Methodist minister and had been a prominent businessman in No Man's Land before coming to this "wild and uncouth country," as he termed it. He held meetings "on the open prairie, in the groves, and anywhere else he could get a crowd together." He soon "enjoyed the best trade in town owing to his complete stock and business methods" and was "conspicuous in all enterprises pertaining to the upbuilding of Ingalls."

Another doctor, J.L. Briggs, arrived in Ingalls with his family of three sons and two daughters. He opened a drugstore south of Sanders' barber shop and established his residence around the corner on Second, back of Perry's.

Across Second from Preacher Perry, William "Old Man" Ransom, the town's wealthiest citizen, and his bartender-partner, Neil D. Murray, constructed a one-room saloon with a full-length bar and poker tables. On the next lots south, Ransom added a livery stable, operated by George Ransom, for the convenience of the saloon's customers.

On the southeast corner of the intersection, Jesse Denton "Dent" Ramsey built another frame structure with a false front lettered HARDWARE. Ramsey was from Ten-

nessee. His father had been killed by lightning when Dent
was three. It had been a struggle for his widowed mother
to feed her children, so at age twelve, Dent bade her good-
bye at Nashville and set out to seek his fortune in the
western territories. He was a straight, slender youth, with
black eyes and hair that revealed his Indian blood bestowed
by the marriage of a Cherokee girl to a grandfather who
came to America from Scotland. Though he never had the
opportunity of learning music, he always owned a fiddle
which he played by ear. At social gatherings, he would
saw out, long and lustily, tunes like "Green Corn," "Small
Potatoes in the Sandy Land," and "Sweet Betsy from
Pike."

Dent had fiddled and traded his way through Arkansas,
Kansas, and Missouri, tried various small business
ventures—a barber shop, saloon, and whiskey distillery—
and married a pretty farm girl, Paulina Seaton, who bore
him a daughter, Maude, and two sons, James Oscar and
Aurora Lee "Arlie," before coming to Oklahoma in 1889.
Dent had obtained a claim immediately south of Ingalls
and, like Preacher Perry, began searching for opportunities
besides raising a few crops to feed his horses and two milch
cows. He became a storekeeper, selling guns and ammunition to cowboys and hardware and farm implements to the
settlers. He also engaged in the real estate business, "looking out for the welfare of parties expecting to locate in a
new and thriving town."

Dr. Duncan Hyder "D.H." Selph and wife Nancy
Elizabeth, with a brother William B. Selph, his wife Ten-
nie and two young sons, Harry and Ernest J., also came
from Tennessee, where D.H. had earned degrees in both
law and medicine. D.H. had chosen medicine, and set up
practice in his residence on Second, across from Doctor
Call's home. William opened a grocery store on Second,
east of Ramsey's hardware, and built a home sided by a
large storm cave a block south of the store and west of Old
Man Ransom's residence on Third.

Three more businesses were established on the east side
of Ash from First to Second: Joe Ketchum's boot shop,
Charley Vaughn's saloon, and William M. Wagner's

blacksmith shop—in that order. Ketchum had been a saddle master with the Seventh U.S. Cavalry. In his shop he
exhibited numerous souvenirs and relics gathered during
his years in the service. Wagner had shod horses for the
Halsell brothers on the Cimarron before the Unassigned
Lands were opened. He built his home half a block east
of his shop and west of Doctor Selph's office, on Second.

Some 100 feet east of the blacksmith shop and across
from Wagner's home, Henry Pierce and his wife, Mary,
constructed the only two-story building in Ingalls—the
O.K. Hotel, managed by Mrs. Pierce and allegedly financed
by Old Man Ransom. There was a storage cellar at the rear,
in front of the kitchen door, and a small dining area off
the ground floor entrance.

The Pierces had hoped to corner the trade of the reservation ranches, but realized their mistake when a woman
named Thomas put in a restaurant north of Perry's dry
goods. They stopped construction on the hotel's upper
floor, which remained an attic, partitioned by curtains and
neither ceilinged nor plastered. It had a window in the
north gable and two windows in the false-fronted gable on
the south. Furnished with bunks, chairs, and a table, it was
used by cowboys who occasionally spent the night in town.

Mary Pierce finished a very comfortable quarters in the
downstairs southeast corner of the building, where she
lived with her two children. She "responded to all activities in town" and "entertained often and quite
lavishly." But the hotel was strictly a place for sleeping
and having a good meal. It was no brothel, as some have
claimed.

Such diversions were provided at another establishment
on Second between the hotel and Wagner's presided over
by Sadie Comley, nee McClaskey.

Sadie was the widow of John Comley, an old Bar X Bar
cowboy killed in a saloon brawl. Two brothers, Oak and
Matthew McClaskey, ran a sawmill east of Ingalls and lived
with their mother southeast of the townsite. Sadie operated
a small gaming parlor and "always kept three or four girls
around." She often dashed about the countryside in a
plumed hat and fancy rig behind a team of high-stepping

Diary of Dr. Jacob Hiram Pickering, 1893–98.

bays and was remembered by old-timers as "Belle of the Cimarron."

In the spring of 1893, Dr. Jacob Hiram Pickering brought his wife, Charlotte Ann, and four children from Nebraska and became the town's fourth and leading physician. The Pickering children were Warney John, Mary Emily "Mollie," Iva May, and LeRoy, ages eighteen, sixteen, twelve, and ten, respectively. A fifth child, Earl Otto, would be born the following November. Pickering's home and office faced Oak Street, at Second, south of the Wilson store and residence.

The doctor apparently had a view to the future, for he began keeping a diary of life in the town. His first entry states, "June 1. Came to Ingalls & bought of Mrs. Thomas our present home, consideration $380.00. Hired Wm. Yowl to drill well."

Ingalls had plenty of good drinking water. A town well was located in the center of the intersection of Ash and Second, with a hand pump and a rough watering trough hewed from a large cottonwood log.

A gristmill and small granary, located on Second between Perry's dry goods and Doctor Briggs' residence, did good business. At that point of the town's development, plans were being made for constructing a cotton gin, a flour mill of fifty barrels daily capacity, and a church.

Education for the young was not neglected. A man named Harry Breece taught a subscription school in the summer of 1890. The first "certificate teacher" appointed was Miss Nevada "Vada" Couch, a Missouri native, who had attended the Worcester Academy established in the Cherokee Nation about 1880 by the American Home Mission Society of New York. Miss Couch had taught for two years at Adair, Cherokee Nation, before accompanying her widowed mother to a claim her brother had staked three and a half miles south of Ingalls in 1889. She taught her first term—January, February, and March of 1891—in a vacant building that stood on the forty acres Shaftsbury had won in his contest suit. Forty-two pupils sat on rough benches made of native lumber to peruse *McGuffy's Reader, Ray's Arithmetic, Barnes' Geography and History,*

Dr. Pickering's home at Ingalls, before the outlaw battle of 1893.

and *Harvey's Grammar.*

Miss Couch's salary was thirty dollars a month. She boarded with an Ingalls family for two dollars a week but soon decided that amount was too much to deduct from her earnings and began riding to and from school on horseback.

A frequent visitor at the school was young George Davis, a Kansas native, who had cowboyed on the Indian reservations since the early 1880s. He had obtained a claim with a good spring about three miles east of Ingalls on Council Creek and built a dugout. Instead of farming, he drove horses and cattle from the ranches and sold them in Oklahoma Territory.

Davis became "struck" on the new schoolmarm and would "drop by" at closing time to accompany her home. "He took me to dances that were held in local homes, visited on Sundays, and helped when there was extra work to be done," Miss Couch recalled. "We held hands and did our courting on horseback." The next year, in 1892, she married Mr. Davis.

Other men holding "fine claims" adjacent to Ingalls and (according to Stillwater's *Oklahoma Hawk* of March 2, 1893) "ever ready to exert their best energies toward the upbuilding of the community in general" were J.A. and Joseph Simmons, John South, William Purcell, James Ashburn, John Irwing, Ernest Chevalier, Ed Strange, John Olin, William Stolling, H. Rhode, H.B. Hardy, Frank McDaniel, H.H. Hammock, W.S. Edmonson, Samuel Steele, B.A. Kelly, Scott Rowden, Clay Wendall, Dock and Russ Ramsey, James Duncan, William Thoe, Robert VanArsdale, and William B. Dunn (alternately referred to as Bill, B., or Bee).

VanArsdale had been engaged in the logging business in the Creek Nation before making the 1889 run and staking a claim in the big bend of the Cimarron near the Simmons family. There was a crossing on the river at his new logging camp, and according to J.N. Fallis, a cousin who worked there through September of 1893, he "kept open house for anyone using the crossing—deputy U.S. marshals and outlaws alike." VanArsdale and the McClaskey sawmill supplied many of the joists and beams for Ingalls residences and business houses.

Bee Dunn had a farm and livestock operation southeast of Ingalls on Council Creek, near the Pawnee reservation border. His original home was a story-and-a-half log structure on a high slope overlooking the creek, with a large, plank-covered storm cave nearby. He soon built a frame house and other good improvements on the ranch with money allegedly not always obtained by honest means. Bee had four brothers—John (the eldest), Dal, George, and Calvin (the youngest)—and a thirteen-year-old sister, Rosa (called Rose). Their father was dead; their mother had married Doctor Call. Rosa lived in Ingalls with her mother.

Two community "upbuilders" not mentioned by the *Hawk* were Robert McGinty of Kansas who, with his sons William "Billy," John, and Isaac, had homesteaded two miles north of Ingalls, and Martin Edgar "Ed" Williams, also of Kansas, who brought his wife and two children to his claim a couple of miles west of the townsite in October of 1889. The McGintys raised hogs and horses; the Williams family poultry, cattle, and "peaches by the barrel." Both families thrived and would remember much of what transpired during the town's "outlaw years."

For Ingalls was not the peaceful, unassuming, and happy spot that it seemed to be.

The *Stillwater Gazette* of July 8, 1892, observed: "A tidal wave of criminality is sweeping the territory. There is scarcely a county that is not the scene of bloodshed, rape and robbery. . . . Some of the thieves and highwaymen are apprehended and made to pay the penalty for their crimes. But the punishment of those who fall into the hands of the law does not prevent others from giving loose reins to passion and committing the gravest offenses. . . .

"Last Saturday afternoon [July 2] another bloody chapter was added to the already dark record of Payne County. . . ."

John I. Anderson, a laborer at the McClaskey sawmill, was preparing to move Robert Leach and his wife from the mill grounds to the Sac and Fox country. Matthew McClaskey borrowed one of Anderson's horses to ride into

Ingalls, promising to return shortly. When McClaskey failed to do so, Anderson went to Ingalls after his horse and found McClaskey drunk. Anderson took his horse and returned to the mill. McClaskey, in a foul mood, arrived soon afterward. He went into a building in the mill yard, reappeared with a revolver, "walked up to Anderson...and shot him down." McClaskey then fled to his mother's home two miles southeast. He was arrested Sunday morning by Constable George W. Perry of Stillwater, and lodged in the Payne County jail.

A coroner's jury found that "the shot fired by McClaskey penetrated Anderson's breast about an inch and a half to the right of the left nipple...ranged upward through the upper lobe of the heart.... There were powder burns on the flesh and clothing. Death was instantaneous." McClaskey was arraigned before Justice of the Peace P.M. Eyler of Stillwater, remanded to jail, and indicted by a grand jury for murder on August 16.

The case was set for the November term of district court, which was to have begun on the first of the month. However, the Hon. Edward B. Green, the presiding judge, failed to attend and sent an order from another county, by mail, directing adjournment until November 10. On November 10 the judge was again absent. The clerk undertook to adjourn the court until Friday, November 11. The judge appeared on that date, convened court, and suspended proceedings for the weekend.

Monday was spent in securing a jury. Presentation of the evidence commenced on November 16. Witnesses provided pertinent details of the case, briefly as follows:

> *Robert Leach:* Am 23 years old.... Saw Mat McClaskey coming from Ingalls, a little over half a mile... saw him next at my house—a dugout, about four feet in the ground... north of the mill.... Council Creek runs in a southeasterly course close by.... When I rode up, Mat [and Anderson were] standing between five and ten feet south of the house. I tied my mule, walked around my buggy... was ten or fifteen feet from Mat when he fired the shot.... Mat [then] turned to me and said, "Stop, Bob, or I will shoot you." I asked him what

was the matter and told him I was the best friend he had. . . . Mat said "I have got to get out of here," and ran.

Mrs. Lilly Leach: Am 17 years old. . . . Saw defendant the morning of July 2. . . gave me his gun and asked me to keep it till he came back from town. . . . When he returned he asked for the gun. . . saw him next in mill yard. . . talking [to Anderson] and whirling his revolver on his finger. . . just before firing. Anderson fell and I ran off and did not. . . see what Mat did.

Constable George W. Perry: Arrested McClaskey [at home] early the morning of July 3. . . handed me the gun. . . said it was the gun he killed Anderson with. . . but not telling why. [Identifies weapon on exhibit.] The revolver is in the same condition as when I got it.

Edward Chapple: Saw Mat McClaskey in In-galls. . . heard him say he would shoot the heart out of Anderson.

Mr. Dodd: I went to the jail to have a talk with Mat on Sunday after July 2. . . asked him if he intended to kill [Anderson] and he said he did.

The prosecution rested. The defense attempted to prove that the killing was "purely accidental":

Matthew McClaskey: Am 26 years old. . . was raised up with Anderson. . . never had any trouble with him. . . went to Ingalls [the morning of July 2] after some salt. . . left my gun in care of Mrs. Leach. . . . After I returned from Ingalls I went in the house and got my gun. . . found John Anderson at the mill site. . . . We were talking and I was whirling my gun on my finger. . . as I whirled it I cocked it and it went off. . . . My brother [Oak McClaskey] had the gun about a week before. . . . I did not know that the gun was broken.

William Sapp: Oak McClaskey, my brother John and myself went out one Sunday to shoot at a mark. Oak shot first. I shot next and my brother John third. When Oak went to shoot the last time, the gun went off accidentally. I did not examine the revolver but Oak did and he said it would not stand cocked.

James Dickerson: Am a gunsmith. . . . The reason [the revolver] would not stay cocked was that one side of the "dog" was worn off.

The jury received the case at six o'clock Thursday evening, and after deliberating all night returned a verdict of guilty. When the verdict was read in court, the prisoner "broke down entirely." Judge Green overruled motions for a new trial and sentenced McClaskey to imprisonment at hard labor in the Lansing, Kansas, penitentiary for life.

"The case has excited great interest and the public are generally satisfied with the result," said the Gazette. It was far from ended, however.

A Guthrie law firm, C.R. Buckner & Sons, filed a writ of habeas corpus in the territorial supreme court, citing a precedent wherein "the failure of the judge to appear and open court upon the day appointed resulted in the loss of the term, and proceedings had by a court at a time not authorized by law are absolutely void." There was then no Oklahoma statute providing for the adjournment of the court by the clerk or other of its officers in case of nonattendance of the judge. "The presence of the judge at the time appointed by law for the holding of the court was indispensable to the validity of the subsequent proceedings, and he had no authority, by order made in another county, to authorize or direct the ministerial officers to exercise judicial powers in opening and adjourning court." All supreme court justices concurred.

McClaskey was released from the Kansas prison to the custody of the Payne County sheriff to answer the charges for which he was originally indicted. He was retried in 1894, convicted of manslaughter in the first degree, and sentenced to twelve years.

More blood was shed on June 29, 1893—the result, according to the Gazette and Guthrie's Oklahoma State Capital, of an "old feud" between Ernest Chevalier and another Ingalls youth, Elijah "Lige" Samples.

In the summer of 1892, Samples "seduced and openly lived with Chevalier's sister Julia," and when forced to marry her, he "swore vengeance against Chevalier." Some time afterwards a quarter of beef was stolen from an Ingalls shop and found in a crib on Samples' place, where Abe Chevalier, Ernest's brother, was living. Samples furnished "some plausible information" that Chevalier had stolen the meat and brought it to the house during the night; that he, Samples, was sleeping upstairs and saw him "cutting it up and salting it away." Chevalier was arrested, given a preliminary hearing before Justice of the Peace Eyler at Stillwater, and released for lack of evidence. "Every fair minded man was convinced that Samples and some other parties not on good terms with Chevalier did the stealing and were trying to clear their own skirts."

On June 27, 1893, Chevalier became postmaster at Ingalls, replacing J.W. Ellsworth. Samples and his followers "talked about getting up a remonstrance against the appointment." Chevalier, "feeling pretty good over the appointment," gave an ice cream social for his friends and went to Samples' place to invite him and Julia and "see if they could not bridge over the old feeling of hatred."

He found Samples in the barn. Samples claimed that Chevalier "said nothing about his good intentions," but asked him what he was going to do about the appointment; that he told Chevalier in "no gentle terms" it was none of his business, drew his revolver, and ordered him off the place; that Chevalier "put his hand to his breast pocket as though to pull a gun." In fact, Chevalier "had nothing in his pocket but a small penknife."

Samples fired, the ball striking Chevalier below the heart. "Ernest turned, when Samples fired twice more, one shot striking below the right shoulder, ranging upward and making a flesh wound. The other struck him in the back of the head, burying itself in the brain. Ernest died almost instantly."

Ingalls citizens arrested Samples and turned him over to Payne County Undersheriff H.A. "Hi" Thompson, who "hurried him off to Stillwater to escape the vengeance of the people." A coroner's jury, headed by A.B. Querry,

Ingalls, O.T., 1893, looking southeast.

found the killing "was wilful and felonious"; a district court jury found Samples guilty of manslaughter in the first degree, and he was sentenced to four years in prison.

Ingalls also was blemished by quackery and livestock thievery. The *Gazette*, in December of 1892, reported that J.W. Ellsworth had "lost four head of horses since coming to Oklahoma," adding, "There are numerous instances of a similar kind. . . in this county this year"; and Doctor Pickering recorded in his diary:

> In April 1893 there came to Ingalls a notorious old quack representing himself to be a physician of 40 yr Experience and a preacher in the Campbelite church. He began preaching for them. Mr. Culburtson also preached for the same church & he called on Bro Johnson to treat his wife for some disability. The Dr. continued to make regular trips 2 & 3 a day. After the sister was able to work in the garden Culbertson ordered him [Johnson] to quit calling as the people was making a public talk. . . . About this time a man by name Cunningham moved to town. He was a great temperance worker & as great a rascal. Johnson & him was soon pulling together. They organized a temperance Lodge and of course Sister C[ulbertson] was a member. Then it was made very hot for old

man Culbertson. Him & his wife had frequent quarrels.
Finally they compromised. He deeded the property to
her & the deeds were not to be recorded unless he died
before she did. If she was to have it done she was to stay
away from Johnson & his following, but in the absence
of Culbertson his wife took the deeds & gave them to
Johnson who took them to Stillwater & had them
recorded. When this was done she told him [Culbertson]
he had no right there & could go. But he did not go. He
worked easy and commenced to investigate the character
of Dr. Johnson and his wife. He showed them up in a
fearful shape by sworn statements & court records that
they had lived in adultery & she had been in jail for same.
The old Dr was given a chance to reply to same pledg-
ing his word & honor (he never had any) that he would
conduct the meeting in a gentlemanly manner. There
was quite a crowd present. He made no defense but at
the close motioned to his wife who had got just back of
Mr. Culbertson & she commenced to hit him on the head
with a loaded whip. Cunningham & a man name of Crow
grabbed Culbertson & held him down until parties forced
them away. There was strong talk of lynching Cunningham & I guess it would of been done if he hadn't
skipped out. The rest gave up & gave bonds. Mrs.
Johnson pled guilty and was fined $10 & costs. Johnson

& Crow...called for separate trials. Crow's came up
first. Everyone thinks the jury was packed. He was ac-
quitted....Johnson continued his case to Dist.
Court...[it was] thrown out by prosecuting att who is
a populist & personal friend of the deft.

Though competitive Cushing grew rapidly, Ingalls remained the magnet for cowboys from the Flat Iron country and Pawnee reservation. Old-time bartender Leamon
Myers, a former cowboy on the XIT ranch of Texas who
worked for Ransom and Murray, recalled that whiskey was
"plentiful." The saloon owners bought their supplies
through a salesman, and it was "quite an expedition to
bring in four and five wagonloads at a time." Beer came
in sixteen-gallon kegs, whiskey in bottles of all sizes.
Whiskey sold for a dime a shot, a big glass of beer the same
price. "Everybody took their whiskey straight, but we had
a big keg of ice water for anybody needing a chaser."

There were "a lot of fights," Myers recounted, but it was
not the cowboys who got "fist happy" after a few drinks.
It was the country boys who came in from the farms.
"They'd get likkered up and have at it." It was also a "fine
joke" to shoot glasses off the bar top, which had to be
"planed down once in a while to remove the bullet marks."

The cowboy crowd had their fun in other ways. "One
time they did get a little boisterous"—rode through town
and made every merchant close shop and come into the
street, then "herded them like cattle into the saloon and
said, 'Give 'em whatever they want to drink.'" Those who
did not imbibe "had to anyway," including a preacher,
who "drank it down, too."

In May 1893, twenty-nine residents and legal voters of
Ingalls filed application with the board of county commissioners to incorporate the townsite, with the view of elect-
ing a mayor and other officials to establish local law and
order. If the application was approved, the record has been
lost.

By that time, the town had become a "pop-off valve"
for Bill Doolin and his long riders. Forced to avoid other
settlements between their robberies, the Wild Bunch could
"blow off the lid" in Ingalls—owned the town.

PRINCIPALS AND THE PLAYERS 2

WILLIAM "BILL" DOOLIN was born in 1858 on a farm in northeastern Johnson County, Arkansas, the son of a sharecropper, Michael "Mack" Doolin, and Artemina Beller. Mack Doolin had met Artemina and married her after moving with his four children—a son and three daughters—from adjoining Newton County following the death of his first wife, Mary, in 1850. Artemina bore him another child, a daughter named Tennessee, in 1859. In 1860, the Doolins bought a forty-acre farm on the Big Piney River in Pilot Rock Township, thirty-five miles northeast of the county east of Clarksville. The land was level and fertile; timbered peaks of the Ozarks rose on every side; the mountain streams abounded with fish; and game was plentiful.

Mack Doolin died in 1865, and Bill grew to manhood helping his mother and the other children run the farm. He received no formal education, but became an expert with a saw and an ax, cutting firewood, making fence posts, and hewing logs for buildings. He also became an expert with a rifle, and there was always meat in the family larder. In 1881, at age twenty-three, he was six feet two inches tall, strikingly slender at 150 pounds, with thick auburn hair, gander-like pale blue eyes, a brindled mustache that practically covered his canine teeth and straight mouth,

27

and a magnetic personality that seemed to overshadow his illiteracy and backwoods crudeness.

Stories of great opportunities in the West were on the lips of everybody in 1881. Bill went to Fort Smith, where he spent a few days and finally signed on with a freight outfit bound for Caldwell, an end-of-track town on the Kansas frontier. He was still in Caldwell in 1882, when he met Texas cattleman Oscar D. Halsell. Oscar and his brother, Harry H. Halsell, had just established a new ranch in the Unassigned Lands.

The Halsells were prominent in North Texas. As the cattle industry grew following the Civil War, they, like many other ranchers, rode the Chisholm Trail drives, crossing and recrossing the Oklahoma country, searching east and west of the trail for new grass on which to graze their herds. Range camps had sprung up in the Cherokee Outlet, the Chickasaw Nation, the reservations of the Plains tribes, and especially in the Unassigned Lands. The Halsells had selected 10,000 lush, spreading acres in the elbow of the Cimarron River northeast of Guthrie called Cowboy Flat. Oscar's cattle were branded HX, Harry's $\frac{HH}{H}$.

Oscar had come to Caldwell for supplies. He took an immediate liking to the energetic young man from Arkansas who could use a saw and an ax—something his cowboys could not do—and put him to work on Cowboy Flat building corrals and constructing two sixteen-by-twenty-foot headquarters dugouts, roofed and lined with split cedar logs, for the cold winter ahead.

Doolin took to the range life like a duck to water and soon became a top hand. Oscar Halsell taught him to read and write well enough to keep the ranch books and, though recognizing a wild streak in Doolin, considered him trustworthy and often sent him to Caldwell and to Texas on ranch business.

During the next few years, Doolin slept under the stars and stood night guard with most of the cowboys who later became notorious members of the Dalton Gang and the Wild Bunch—Alfred George Newcomb, Richard L. "Dick" Broadwell, William F. Raidler, William Tod Power, and Richard West.

"Little Bill" Raidler.

Newcomb had spent his early years at Fort Scott, Kansas, where his father was associated with one of the largest wholesale grocery establishments in the state. In 1878, when Newcomb was twelve, Charlie Slaughter, a Texas cowman whose Long S ranch lay at the headwaters of the Colorado River, delivered a herd of ponies at Fort Scott. When Slaughter left, Newcomb went with him and was afterward known as "Slaughter's Kid." Subsequently he drove cattle on the Chisholm Trail and was employed by Oscar Halsell. He liked to celebrate in the Kansas border towns and became known as "Bitter Creek" because he was always chanting the lines of that familiar range-country boast, "I'm a bad man from Bitter Creek, and it's my night to howl!"

Broadwell also hailed from Kansas. His brother was a salesman for a tea company and his brother-in-law a grocer in Hutchinson. Somewhat a drinker and gambler, he traveled under the aliases "John Moore" and "Texas Jack." He could "ride, rope and shoot with the best of 'em," and was considered a "valuable hand."

Raidler was twenty-eight years old, small of stature, of good Pennsylvania Dutch ancestry, and well-educated. The cattle ranges early fascinated him, and he had worked for the Halsells several years before coming to Cowboy Flat. He became known as "Little Bill" to distinguish him from big Bill Doolin.

Little is known of William Power except that he ran away from home and a stepmother in Pulaski County, Missouri, at age thirteen. He first appeared on Cowboy Flat with a trail herd from the Pecos and worked for the Halsells in 1888. Using the alias "Tom Evans," he was always ready for a wild exploit and thoroughly enjoyed riding to some Kansas border town with the HX bunch to "paint 'er bright red."

West, called "Little Dick" to distinguish him from Dick Broadwell, never told of his origins, except that he once said, "I was just dropped on the prairie somewhere. Ma died soon after, an' pa broke his life-long rule about sleepin' under a roof. He got caught, an' I ain't seen him since." West was a spindle-legged waif, washing dishes in a Decatur, Texas, greasy-spoon restaurant when picked up on the streets in 1881 by the foreman of the Three Circle ranch and taken to Clay County to wrangle horses. In the spring of 1882, Oscar Halsell employed him to bring his remuda north to Cowboy Flat. He was then sixteen, "wild as a cat and full of cussedness," ate his meals away from the others and, summer or winter, always slept in the open. He left the Halsells in 1888, drifting into the Osage Nation, where he worked at odd jobs and lived in a "secret" cave, later used as a hideout when he became an outlaw.

That same year the government ordered all cattlemen out of the Unassigned Lands. The Halsells moved east into the Iowa reservation, and finally into the Cherokee Nation. Not all of their cowboys accompanied them; some "soonered" on the Cimarron.

Bill Power got a homestead, sold the relinquishment for $1,200, and went to the Flat Iron country to work on the Bar X Bar. Newcomb obtained a claim which he relinquished for a like profit and went to the Sac and Fox country to work on the Turkey Track.

Broadwell was not so lucky. A pretty young widow won a claim near his choice quarter-section on Cowboy Flat, and he found himself deeply in love. She agreed to marry him but did not wish to live on a farm. She had taken the claim only as an investment. She persuaded him to sell both quarter sections and go with her to Fort Worth. At Fort Worth, he kept enough money to buy a new suit to get married in. He put the rest in her care, with instructions to buy the marriage license and open a bank account. The girl disappeared with the money, and Broadwell never saw her again. He returned briefly to his Kansas home. When next heard from, he had joined Power on the Bar X Bar.

Doolin left the Halsells in the Iowa reservation to become "second boss" on the Bar X Bar. Among the cowboys was a fuzz-faced lad named Emmett Dalton, who branded calves, wrangled horses, and rode line near the Pawnee agency. For a few months, he and Doolin were saddle companions.

In the fall of 1888, Doolin was employed by the Wyeth
Cattle Company, which had pastures along Black Bear
Creek in the Oto-Missouri reservation. He occasionally appeared in Arkansas City with the Wyeth crowd "to take
the town apart" but was reportedly the "most peaceful man
in the outfit."

Tom Waggoner of Texas, who grazed his herds in both
the Oto-Missouri reservation and the Unassigned Lands,
leased 60,000 acres in the Osage Nation, and in the spring
of 1889, moved 15,000 cattle across the Arkansas to his
new 3-D ranch, spreading east from Hominy Creek to Wild
Cat Hill, west of Sperry. Tom Humpreys, the 3-D foreman,
brought with him from the Oto "some of the best cowboys
who ever trailed a rein in front of a cow pony," including
Doolin and a husky, dark-faced, heavily mustached youth,
William Blake.

Blake spent much of his time around the gaming tables
in nearby Tulsa and became known as "Tulsa Jack." After
a brief stay at the 3-D, he gave up cowboy life to work for
the railroad in Rice County, Kansas.

Doolin returned to the Bar X Bar.

Billy McGinty, a line rider on the Bar X Bar at that time,
remembered Doolin well. Billy had begun his cowboy
career in 1885, at age fourteen, on the Mack Mann ranch
southeast of Dodge City, ridden for the Comanche Pool,
in the Outlet, and "rounded up wild heifers" for the Dia-
mond Slash outfit in the rough gypsum bluffs of Barber
County, Kansas, before coming to the Flat Iron country.

Billy recalled:

> The Bar X Bar pasture was one of the largest. . . . Its
> southern boundary ran seventy-five miles along the
> Cimarron. My partner was John Comley, who married
> Sadie McClaskey and got himself killed. . . . Our camp
> was at the mouth of Council Creek. John rode the fence
> line north and I rode the fence line east twenty-five miles
> and return. We made the trip every day, making each
> of us ride fifty miles. We watched the fence and kept
> it repaired. If any cattle broke through we had to trail
> them and bring them back to the home pasture. John
> McClain was the foreman. . . told me they pastured

80,000 head that year.

I also worked with Bill Doolin, unloading steers at Red Fork station [a spur on the Frisco railroad that had been built from Vinita, Cherokee Nation, to Tulsa to get the cattle business in the area]. Doolin was sort of a slow fellow, grinned a little, but a real comedian when he got started. His big hands would wrap almost twice around the butt of a six-shooter, and he was a crack shot. . . .

I left the Bar X Bar when my father came down from Kansas to make the run in '89. I was too young to take a claim, but knew a good spot west of Council Creek. . . . After the run I stayed with father on his claim for a while, then went to Pond Creek to work for the A66. The A66 sent me to their ranch in Texas, and I did not see Doolin again until 1893. He had been wounded by a posse after robbing a train in Kansas.

Doolin was still on the Bar X Bar in 1890. According to Jim Williams, a horse wrangler on the Bar X Bar for many years, Doolin "got into his first real trouble" on the Fourth of July, at Coffeyville:

> There was a three-day celebration going on and some of the cowboys decided to hold a celebration of their own up in the timber about a quarter of a mile. [Kansas was a dry state and alcoholic beverages were illegal.] They had barrels sawed in two and filled with ice and beer bottles. There was a keg besides, and everybody could have all he wanted. After drinking their first bottle. . . each took a second and were in a circle standing around.
>
> Then a couple of constables appeared and asked who owned the beer. Doolin was always the spokesman of his crowd and everybody waited for him to answer. He said, "Why, that beer don't belong to anyone. It's free, gentlemen, help yourselves."
>
> The officers said that if they could not find the owners they would take the beer anyway. Bill said, "Don't try to take the beer. . . ." The men started to roll the keg away, a gunfight started, and both constables were badly wounded. Whether Bill fired the shots or not was never proved, but as the leader he was considered responsible. From then on he had to be on the dodge.

A warrant was issued for Doolin but was never served. Oscar Halsell had disposed of his cattle interests, opened a livery stable in Guthrie, and formed a wholesale grocery enterprise with Evett Dumas Nix under the firm name of Nix and Halsell Company, supplying trading points throughout the territory and in the Osage Nation. During the winter of 1890–91, Doolin worked at the Halsell livery stable. In the spring of 1891, he was back on the Cimarron with Broadwell, Power, and Newcomb, and palling around with two new acquaintances—Charley Pierce and "Black-Faced Charley" Bryant.

Charley Pierce (not related to the Pierce family of Ingalls) was a sorry character—scowling, thick-chested, long-haired, and tobacco chewing. He was a native of the Blue River country of Missouri, where his drunken sprees and burglarizing of local homes had exhausted the patience of the citizenry and his disgraced family. Then he got a girl pregnant. Her angry clansmen declared they had no use for him as kinfolk, even by the grace of a shotgun wedding. While they were oiling their weapons, Pierce escaped to the Indian Nations on a fine racing stallion furnished by his brother. He found refuge on the Pawnee reservation, where he raced his stallion and did right well until caught selling whiskey to the Indians. He was given a stiff sentence in the federal jail at Fort Smith. Banned from the Pawnee country, after his release, he had sought employment on the Turkey Track.

Bryant—rail-thin, beady-eyed, and sinister looking—had come from Wise County, Texas, to assist in the last round-ups and removal of Turkey Track herds from the Sac and Fox reservation, preparatory to the opening of 1892. He fought like a wildcat, was lightning fast with a six-shooter, and had killed men. In one pistol duel at close quarters, exploding gunpowder had burned his face, leaving a large black splotch over his left cheek, hence his appellation. He suffered from a ravaging fever that came on often, leaving him deathly sick and pale. During one feverish attack, he boasted, "I want to get killed—in one hell-firin' minute of smoking action!"

He would shortly get his wish.

During Ingalls' struggle to exist, Doolin and his cronies patronized the early merchants and made many friends in the vicinity. They traded horses and bought much of their gear at Beal's General Store and Corral. Doctor Call "concocted remedies for their illnesses," and Doctor Selph "treated them many times when they were sick or injured." Joe Vickrey shod their mounts at Falls City. Sherm Sanders did "all their barber work" and was "paid well" for his services. Bee Dunn was on "very friendly terms" with Doolin, Newcomb, and Pierce; they often put up at his old log house on Council Creek. They bought milk and eggs from the settlers and attended dances and other functions. One old-timer claimed (however unlikely) that one evening Doolin donned a blue serge suit and made a talk at the local literary society!

Doolin's chief interest at Ingalls was Edith Ellsworth, whom he met at a dance and persistently courted during the summer of 1891, while she was clerking at Mrs. McMurtry's notions shop. Bill told her nothing of his Kansas trouble or his intentions for the future. Though she suspected he was "more than a cowboy, a daring rider," his "dashing, debonair way" so attracted her that she "found herself in love with him."

Neither Edith Ellsworth nor Ingalls knew that Doolin already had cast his lot with the Dalton Gang.

ENTER
THE DALTONS 3

THE NUCLEUS OF the Dalton Gang included Bob Dalton, the leader, and two of his brothers, Grat and Emmett. Their parents were James Lewis Dalton, Jr., and Adeline Lee Younger, daughter of Charles Younger and a half-sister to Henry Washington Younger, father of Coleman, Bob, Jim, and John, who associated themselves with Jesse and Frank James and gained notoriety as the James-Younger gang following the Civil War.

James Lewis Dalton, Jr., was born in Montgomery County, Kentucky, February 16, 1826. The following year his family moved to Jackson County, Missouri. At age twenty, in 1846, he was back in Montgomery County, Kentucky, where he joined the army at Mount Sterling on May 25. He served in the Mexican War as a fifer in Company I, Second Kentucky Infantry, and was mustered out at New Orleans, Louisiana, June 6, 1847. In 1851 he returned to Missouri and married sixteen-year-old Adeline Younger. Charles Younger died soon afterward, leaving Adeline some two hundred acres of land in Cass County, where she and James Lewis moved in 1852.

Emmett Dalton, in his books *Beyond the Law* (1918) and *When the Daltons Rode* (1931), lists fifteen Dalton children. U.S. census reports, death certificates, and other official records show their names and years of birth as follows: Charles Benjamin "Ben," 1852; Henry Coleman "Cole," 1853; Lewis Kossuth, 1855 (died at age seven); Bea Elizabeth, 1856; Littleton Lee "Lit," 1857; Franklin "Frank," 1859; Gratton Hanley "Grat," 1861; William Marion "Bill" (aka Mason Frakes), 1863; Eva May, 1867; Robert Rennick "Bob," 1869; Emmett, 1871; Leona, 1875; Nancy May "Nannie," 1876; Hanna Adeline and Simon Noel (twins), 1878. Hanna Adeline died at birth or a few days thereafter.

The Daltons were never well off financially. James Lewis was a morose, gloomy-looking individual with a love for fast horses and easy living. Before he married he had engaged briefly in the saloon business at Westport Landing (present Kansas City). He had little taste for farming and soon squandered Adeline's inheritance on his horse racing and trading ventures, traveling all over the country in a covered wagon with his brood and his bang-tailed ponies. In 1860, he won two hundred acres of good land near Denver, Colorado, from a gambler and racehorse man, but a few months later loaded his brood into his wagon and drove off and left it.

The family was residing near Lawrence, Kansas, when the Civil War erupted and moved back to Missouri to get away from the bloody struggle between the free-state and pro-slavery factions. The bitter enmity quickly spread the length of the border. Kansas Redlegs and Jayhawkers raided Missouri's western counties; the Quantrill and other guerrilla bands plundered the Kansas abolitionists. Gen. Thomas Ewing, who commanded this center of hostilities, issued his infamous Order No. 10 and Order No. 11, resulting in the arrest of hundreds of pro-Southerners in Jackson, Cass, Bates, and Vernon counties. Almost the entire population of the area was evacuated, including the Daltons.

The war left western Missouri a veritable wasteland. The Daltons moved to a farm near Coffeyville, Kansas, where they lived for the next several years. Bea, the eldest daughter, had married a man named Harrison, from Texas. Harrison died in the early 1870s, and Bea worked in a hotel at Brownsville, where she met and married Tom Phillips, a Texas Ranger, and reared five children. She died in December 1894.

The rest of the Dalton children virtually grew up on the Kansas-Indian Territory border. From there the older brothers, Benjamin, Henry Coleman, and Littleton, migrated to California. They never married and became honest, hard-working citizens. Bill Dalton went to Montana, then to California. He married the daughter of a rancher in Merced County, dabbled in politics, and aspired to become a state senator—a position he never achieved. In 1881, Grat joined Bill on the Pacific Coast.

In 1882, James Lewis moved the rest of the family to the Cherokee Nation, leasing some Indian land near Locust Hill, south of Vinita. As usual, he was away most of the time, following carnivals and county fairs, visiting his older sons, and racing horses on the tracks in California. At Fresno in 1887, broke, he applied for his Mexican War pension.

That same year, Eva May married John Whipple of Meade, Kansas. She lived in Colorado and Arkansas most of the remainder of her life.

Adeline and the rest of the children eked out a living at Locust Hill. Frank helped support the family by riding as deputy marshal for the federal court of Judge Isaac Charles Parker. He was a brave officer and widely respected. In November 1887, he was slain in a gun battle with a gang of horse thieves and whiskey peddlers in the Arkansas River bottoms west of Fort Smith.

Frank's death was a blow to his friends and family. Grat came back from California to fill his boots. Grat was twenty-seven, tall, blond, with faded blue eyes—an "inveterate card player...fond of whiskey," and prone to take chances. In 1888, he was wounded in the left forearm while attempting to arrest a notorious Indian desperado. In 1889, he was commissioned deputy marshal for the new federal court in Indian Territory at Muskogee.

Bob Dalton, now nineteen, found employment as an Indian policeman for the Osage agency at Pawhuska. He also served as deputy under United States Marshal William C.

Jones of the Judicial District of Kansas, bringing many small-fry bootleggers to the federal court at Wichita. Early in 1889, Emmett left the Bar X Bar to ride with Bob and Grat as a posseman.

James Lewis—the Locust Hill project soured—took his wife and remaining children back to Missouri, working at odd jobs for a time. In 1890, they left Missouri in a covered wagon for a new start in Oklahoma Territory. While traveling through southeastern Kansas, James Lewis suffered an attack of cholera morbus. On July 16, he died unexpectedly at the home of a friend near Dearing and was buried in the Robbins Cemetery west of Coffeyville.

Adeline, with Nannie, Leona, and Simon, continued the journey to Oklahoma and found a tract of land six miles northeast of Kingfisher, where they lived in a dugout at first, then in a log cabin. When the Cheyenne-Arapaho reservation was opened for settlement in 1892, Adeline secured a homestead ten miles farther west, on Cooper Creek. Benjamin returned from California to help farm both places. Nannie married Charles M. Clute, who also obtained a claim in the Cheyenne-Arapaho country. Simon served with the army in the Philippine Insurrection of 1899–1901 and married after his discharge in December 1902. Leona remained single and became the mainstay of the family. All were a credit to the community.

Early in 1890, Bob Dalton resigned as Indian policeman because of a "cut in pay" that was "entirely unacceptable." In fact, he was caught selling protection to whiskey peddlers in the Osage, and excused his actions by claiming he had been "beat out" of several hundred dollars in government fees due him for services to the Wichita court. "Bob just decided to get even," Emmett said. His deputy marshal's commission was revoked, and he turned to the outlaw trail.

In June, Bob and Emmett stole several head of ponies and mules in the Osage, disposing of them in the Cherokee Nation and Kansas. They then returned to the vicinity of Claremore, boldly rounded up about thirty horses belonging to some prominent Cherokee citizens, and sold them to a trader at Columbus, Kansas. Closely pursued by the angry owners, they escaped on fresh mounts allegedly furnished by brother Grat and fled to California. Grat was jailed at Fort Smith, but released for lack of evidence. He also lost his deputy's commission, and within a few weeks, joined Bob and Emmett on the Pacific Coast.

The Dalton Gang's first train robbery attempt was on the Southern Pacific railroad near Alila, Tulare County, February 6, 1891. The fireman was wounded and died the next day. Bob and Emmett were traced to Ludlow, a station on the Atlantic & Pacific Railway about a hundred miles east of Mojave, where they disposed of their horses and purchased tickets on an eastbound train. A $5,000 reward was offered by the Southern Pacific Company, in addition to a $300 reward by the state of California and Wells Fargo Express company, for their arrest and conviction. Injured when his horse fell during the ride from Alila, Grat was captured. Bill Dalton, who tried to furnish Grat an alibi and sheltered him, was indicted as an accomplice. Both were jailed at Visalia.

Bob and Emmett reached their mother's home northeast of Kingfisher at the end of April. Word of their California foray preceded them, and they headed for the Flat Iron country, where there were many hideouts and cow-camp friends to keep them posted. En route, they stole fresh mounts from a colony of Missourians near Orlando, in Logan County. The farmers gave pursuit and were ambushed in the Twin Mounds area northwest of Ingalls. Their leader, William Starmer, was slain and another posse member badly wounded.

A hue and cry arose: "Alive or dead—get the Daltons!" But early apprehension was not in the offing. Bitter Creek Newcomb and Black-Faced Charley Bryant joined Bob and Emmett in the Pawnee reservation. On the night of May 9, the quartet held up the Texas Express at Wharton, a cattle shipping station on the Santa Fe railroad thirty miles north of Guthrie, in the Outlet.

According to Emmett, they escaped with a "big haul" of $9,000. The Wells Fargo company minimized the loss at $1,745. Telegraph wires chattered wild messages; railroad detectives, deputy U.S. marshals and their posses combed the Outlet and the Indian reservations—east, north, and south—in one of the greatest manhunts in territorial history; Kingfisher authorities staked out the Adeline Dalton residence; and the press filled its columns with demands for the gang's extermination.

Far west of the search arena, on the ranch of "Big Jim" Riley in the Cheyenne-Arapaho country on the South Canadian River (near present Taloga), the quartet found food and shelter. Riley had known Adeline Dalton and her part of the brood when he was a stage driver between Fort Reno and Caldwell. By 1891 he had married a Cheyenne woman and begun raising horses and cattle. He always denied any part in the gang's operations. Living as he did a hundred miles from a railroad or large settlement, it behooved him to accommodate passersby and attend to his own business. Nonetheless, Emmett considered Riley "one of their most loyal friends."

Fifteen miles from the ranch headquarters, on a high clay bluff above the cedar brakes of the river, the country could be viewed for miles. The gang built a dugout there, "camouflaged with brush and tree branches" and stocked with canned goods, flour, coffee, and beans. Supplemented with wild game in the area, they "fared well" and "worked cattle" for Big Jim during the summer.

Then the Daltons were riding again. They scouted eastward through the cattle ranges along the southern border of the Outlet, carefully avoiding the farming areas and settlements in Oklahoma Territory. Their destination was Wagoner, a hub of activity on the Missouri, Kansas and Texas (Katy) railroad, in the Creek Nation. It was common knowledge that on the fifteenth of each month the railroad carried as much as $25,000 to meet the payrolls of coal companies at Lehigh, Choctaw Nation.

The third day out, Black-Faced Charley Bryant suffered one of his feverish attacks. There was no indication that he would recover soon. His companions left him in a friendly cow camp near Buffalo Springs with instructions where to rejoin them. His condition grew worse. Some of the cowboys persuaded Bryant to let them take him to Hennessey, seven miles south, for medical treatment. A physician examined him and ordered him to bed in the Rock Island Hotel.

Deputy Marshal Ed Short, headquartered at Hennessey, saw Bryant when he was brought in and recognized him as one of the Wharton robbers. He arrested and handcuffed the pain-racked outlaw in his hotel room. On August 23, when Bryant had recovered sufficiently to be moved, Short put him on the Rock Island train for Wichita, where territorial prisoners were kept prior to 1892. Warned that Bryant's companions might try to rescue him, the marshal decided against sitting in the coaches and obtained permission to transport his prisoner in the combination mail and baggage car.

As the train neared Waukomis Station in the Outlet, Short saw several riders coming across the prairie at a rapid clip. Not knowing if they were cowboys who, like the Indians, often were thrilled at the arrival of a locomotive, the marshal, carrying his Winchester, stepped out onto the platform between the baggage car and smoker to better observe the horsemen.

In the car, Black-Faced Charley spotted a revolver inadvertently left by the baggage agent in one of the pigeonholes for sorting letters. He knew that his "hell-firin' minute of smoking action" had come. Short, satisfied that the riders were only cowhands coming for their mail, turned to reenter the car and saw his prisoner, the cocked weapon in his manacled hands, facing him in the vestibule door.

Bryant's shot struck the marshal below the heart. Though mortally wounded, Short threw his rifle to his hip and poured lead into Bryant's body as fast as he could lever and pull the trigger. When the train stopped at Waukomis, outlaw and lawman lay dead on the platform.

With Bryant's demise, Bob Dalton gathered a "more adequate corps of train boarders." Besides Emmett and Newcomb, the gang now included Charley Pierce, Bill Power, Dick Broadwell, and Bill Doolin. Singly and in pairs, they assembled near Wagoner and heard Bob's final instructions. On the afternoon of September 15, the sextet held up the Katy train four miles to the north, at the little cattle-loading station of Leliaetta.

The Lehigh payroll was in a through safe which could not be opened, but the express company's loss from the way safe amounted to $2,500. Each outlaw's divvy was even less than the take at Wharton.

The robbery also marked the first clash between Bob Dalton and Doolin. As they were leaving the express car, several foolhardy passengers emerged from the train to see what the shooting was about. Certain that some of them were carrying firearms and might attempt a "counter-offensive," Doolin cursed and shouted, "Watch me scare hell outa them!" Bob allegedly ordered him to desist, but Doolin mounted his horse and, firing his six-shooter in the air and yelling like a banshee, raced the length of the train and drove everyone back into the coaches.

True or not, that action was not what irritated Bob Dalton. Bill had arrived early at the rendezvous, on September 9, and without Bob's permission had ridden into Wagoner and posed for a studio portrait to be delivered to his sweetheart at Ingalls. A copy of the photo, obtained by Capt. Charley LeFlore of the Indian police, became a link in the chain connecting Bill with the Dalton Gang. Further, Bill declined to accompany Bob and Emmett to the Riley ranch hideout on the South Canadian. He felt safer among his Ingalls friends. Pierce, Power, Broadwell, and Newcomb returned to their respective cow camps on the Cimarron.

In California, Bill Dalton had been released on bail, and eventually would win an acquittal. Grat was convicted for assault with intent to commit robbery at Alila. On the night of September 18, pending filing an appeal to the California supreme court, he and three other prisoners broke jail at Visalia. His companions boarded a freight train at Goshen, and Grat dodged posses in the Sierra foothills for weeks until the hunt died sufficiently for him to slip out of the state and back to Oklahoma Territory.

When and why Grat joined his brothers is problematical. Bob and Emmett worked on Riley's ranch throughout the fall and winter of 1891 and in the spring roundup of 1892. Emmett says Grat "told of his trial and escape," and "the burning within him burst forth''; there was no ''formal word'' that he should join in their foray. ''We were Daltons, and Daltons we would remain to the bitter end.'' Bob had learned that $70,000 in Indian annuity money was to be expressed on June 1 on the Santa Fe to the Sac and Fox agency. ''Toward the end of May'' they ''rendezvoused'' with Doolin, Newcomb, Pierce, Broadwell, and Power in the Pawnee country, and ''got the train'' at Red Rock, an Indian trading post and cattle-loading depot in the Oto-Missouri reservation, twenty-six miles northeast of Wharton.

It was the gang's most daring exploit to date—and the most disappointing. The express messenger and guard extinguished the lights in their car and stood their ground while lead ripped through the wooden walls from every quarter, even from under the car through the floor. Some sixty shots were exchanged before the messenger and guard surrendered. The bandits found only a way safe, which Grat and Doolin ripped open with a sledge hammer and chisel, obtaining less than $2,000. The Sac and Fox money had gone through earlier on a passenger train guarded by a squad of U.S. marshals and Wells Fargo detectives.

The *Stillwater Gazette* of June 10 gives a comprehensive account of the manhunt that followed:

> On June 4 . . . the pursuers were sixty miles west of Red Rock. There were twenty-five deputies in the party . . . . A party has started from Caldwell, Kansas, going south, in sufficient numbers and fully armed, to do battle in case they intercept the fleeing road agents . . . . United States Deputy Marshals [Ransom] Payne and [Chris] Madsen were in the Panhandle country with a posse . . . watching to prevent their escape . . . . The latest reports state that the robbers were on the trail leading to Fort Supply and their pursuers were following them very close. A posse had started from Fort Supply to intercept them.

The *Gazette* of June 17 tells how the manhunt ended:

> All pursuing parties have returned and the chase aban-

doned. Marshals [Frank] Kress and [George] Severns, with eleven others, chased the robbers over two hundred miles before their horses gave out [and it was] no use to go further. They chased the thieves into the Cimarron hills in the strip [Outlet], then south into...the Cheyenne and Arapaho country and finally back into the Cimarron hills.

The thieves had obtained a relay of fresh horses [at the Riley ranch] and it was then very easy for them to ride away from their pursuers.... Four horses which the robbers had abandoned were picked up and brought back by the marshals.

With their ranch hideout in the Cheyenne-Arapaho country known to the marshals and the western ranches of the Outlet swarming with posses and bounty hunters, the gang doubled back through the Oto-Missouri and Pawnee reservations. The Daltons, Broadwell, and Power found refuge in a Creek Nation cave west of Tulsa, which Grat had discovered and used often as a camping place while serving as deputy marshal. Newcomb and Pierce "idled time" at the Dunn ranch on Council Creek, while Doolin visited Edith Ellsworth and other Ingalls acquaintances. The second week of July, the gang reassembled in the Cherokee Nation on Pryor Creek, a few miles west of Pryor Creek Station on the Katy railroad.

Bob's original plan was to rob the Katy express at Pryor Creek Station, but their "bivouac" was discovered July 14 by an Indian farmer looking for some stray hogs. He notified the Pryor Creek agent, as Bob anticipated. By day's end, word had been flashed along the line that the Daltons were in the area. At Muskogee, a special force of railroad detectives, marshals, and Indian police was organized for a "counter surprise." Bob said, "We'll outfox them." On July 15, he led the gang nine miles north and attacked the 9:42 P.M. train at the little farming community of Adair.

According to the July 21 issue of the Vinita *Indian Chieftain*, "they ransacked the station office," made "short work" of the express car, "taking everything they could find, even things of no value to them at all," and wounded two of a half-dozen guards riding in the smoker. Dr. T.S.

Youngblood of Adair, and Dr. W.L. Goff, a visitor from
Missouri, watched the melee from the porch of a store
building sixty-five yards from the track. "As the raiders
were retiring . . . three or four passed through the street
[and] fired a volley of eighteen or twenty shots at these doctors. Both were hit in each leg." Doctor Youngblood's right
foot had to be "taken off at the instep," and one of Doctor
Goff's legs amputated. Doctor Goff died next morning from
"loss of blood." The guards' wounds were dressed and
"all went south on the four o'clock morning train." The
amount of loot obtained was "not learned," but "express
folks say 'very little' as the raid was expected and no
shipments of value were made by the night train."

The gang fled into the Grand River Hills, where Bob,
Grat, and Emmett knew many routes for escape. A few
hours' ride away was their boyhood home at Locust Hill.
The Katy railroad and Pacific Express Company jointly offered $5,000 for "the arrest and conviction" of each rob-
ber. But, as the *Chieftain* reported, "men of experience in
this country who know the Dalton boys know they cannot
be captured alive. To kill them . . . will not secure the
reward. . . . A call for volunteers to make up a pursuing
party met with so few responses the project was
abandoned."

Murder warrants were issued for the gang in the U.S.
commissioner's court at Fort Smith. But the Daltons did
not fear capture by deputy marshals. More disturbing were
the repercussions over the senseless shooting of Doctors
Goff and Youngblood, which even a rough frontier society
with little sympathy for the railroads could not approve.

There was much grumbling as the gang made its way
west from the Grand River Hills into the Caney River country and through the southeast corner of the Osage Nation.
There never had been enough divvy to split eight ways.

At the Creek Nation cave west of Tulsa, Bob, Grat, and
Emmett held a "council of war," in which each member
was appraised in turn. Though short on tact and
shrewdness, Broadwell and Power always followed orders.
Doolin was "unruly." At Adair, he had strutted up and
down the depot platform without the wit to avoid un-

necessary danger. And there was the "dangerous credulity" of Newcomb and Pierce. They, like Doolin, were too fond of hobnobbing with Ingalls citizens and the Dunn boys. Bob told them, "Someday it will cost you your lives." Newcomb bristled, "We ain't no suckin' calves."

The gang was pruned down to Bob, Grat, Emmett, Broadwell, and Power. It was a friendly parting. Bob promised to get in touch should something come to mind. Doolin, Newcomb, and Pierce rode off to their old haunts on the Cimarron.

However streamlined, the Daltons soon found the ground too hot for them to circulate. Within a few weeks after the Adair robbery, five railroad and three express companies that had suffered from their depredations financed an outfit to hunt the gang until they were driven from the country or exterminated. New rewards were offered—$1,000 for each member, dead or alive. Detective Fred Dodge of the Wells Fargo express was placed in charge of field operations.

Dodge began his hunt near Tulsa, along the Arkansas, into the Osage and Cherokee nations. Word was spread that anyone caught "aiding and abetting" the outlaws would be charged in federal court at Fort Smith. The Daltons became "afraid to trust anybody." The action drove them northeastward during August and September, and resulted in Bob's scheme to rob two banks at Coffeyville, Kansas, simultaneously, flee to a certain camp in the Cherokee Outlet, thence northwest to Seattle, Washington, and from there take separate boats for South America.

Doolin, Newcomb, and Pierce were not included in the raid. Bob's proposal, according to Emmett, was a "startling surprise," but "feasible." Having lived near Coffeyville several years, they knew the town's inhabitants and their habits intimately. They knew, too, that both banks were prosperous institutions. "We chose early morning when they would be opening and there would have been no very large withdrawals. . . . Grat, Powers, and Broadwell were to enter the Condon bank. . . Bob and I the First National. We would clean them out, come together, mount and get away." The proceeds would be split five ways.

Then would come the separation. "What Broadwell and Power proposed to do with their share we did not know or care . . . neither were greatly impressed with our idea of leaving the country."

At 9:30 P.M., October 5, the five outlaws—Bob, Grat, and Broadwell wearing false whiskers—rode into the town's plaza. The hitching rails outside the banks had been temporarily removed for street repairs, and they were forced to leave their mounts more than a block away, tied to a board fence in an alley—a circumstance that was to contribute to their undoing. Quickly they formed into a quasi-military line, three in front and two in the rear, and walking closely together. As they emerged from the alley, they passed stableman Aleck McKenna, who was standing in front of his business only a few feet away. McKenna noted their Winchesters and handguns and, despite the disguises, recognized Bob and Grat Dalton. When the first three men darted into the C.M. Condon and Company bank and the two in the rear ran directly across the street into the First National, McKenna began to spread the alarm.

While Bob and Emmett at the First National were forcing cashier Thomas G. Ayers, teller W.H. Sheppard, and bookkeeper Bert S. Ayers to fill a grain sack with currency and gold, townspeople were shouting warnings and arming themselves in the nearby stores. At the Condon, Grat and company confronted vice-president C.T. Carpenter, bookkeeper T.C. Babb, and cashier C.M. Ball with Winchesters. They stuffed their vests with the cash on hand and ordered Ball to bring them the money from the vault. Ball "undertook to parley," claiming that the time lock was set for 9:45 A.M. Grat calmly replied, "That is only three minutes yet—I will wait." Ball tried to appease him by dragging out a bag of silver. At that juncture, a bullet from outside broke the plate glass window, and Grat forgot about the vault. He grabbed up the silver and led his men from the bank, guns blazing.

Bob and Emmett emerged from the First National but were driven back by gunfire. Pushing Sheppard and Bert Ayers before them, they fled out the back door toward the alley. A young man named Lucius Baldwin, armed with

Dalton Gang, in death, after the Coffeyville raid, October 5, 1892. *Left to right:* Bill Power, Bob Dalton, Grat Dalton, and Dick Broadwell.

a pistol, intercepted them and was cut down by Bob's Winchester. Two other brave citizens, George W. Cubine and Charles J. Brown, became Bob's next victims, and cashier Ayers, who had rushed from the bank and obtained a weapon, fell with a ball in the left cheek before the pair reached their horses.

Grat, Broadwell, and Power joined them in the alley, closely pressed by City Marshal Charles T. Connelly, livery stable owner John J. Kloehr, and barber Cary Seamen, pouring a barrage of lead. Grat shot the marshal to death, and Kloehr replied in kind, killing Grat, Power, and Bob Dalton with his Winchester. Emmett caught a slug that broke his right arm. Still clutching the sack of loot, he managed to mount, but was blown from the saddle when a load of buckshot from Seamen's gun struck him in the back and shoulders. Broadwell rode from the alley and escaped amid a deadly fusillade from Kloehr's rifle and Seamen's shotgun. A hastily organized posse followed the bleeding bandit and came upon him a half mile west of town, lying dead in the roadway, his horse standing beside him. He was hauled back to the city in a farm wagon and laid alongside his confederates in crime.

The next afternoon, Broadwell, Power, and Bob and Grat Dalton were buried at city expense in Elmwood Cemetery. Later, Broadwell's body was claimed by relatives and reinterred at Hutchinson. Emmett Dalton survived his wounds. He was charged with bank robbery and two counts of murder, convicted of second degree murder in the death of George Cubine, and given a life sentence in the state penitentiary at Lansing. He married while in prison, was pardoned in 1907, and moved to California, where he engaged in real estate, wrote his memoirs, and dabbled in motion pictures until his death in 1937.

The Dalton Gang hardly had been exterminated. Down on the Cimarron, Doolin, Newcomb, and Pierce thanked their lucky stars that they had not been included in the disaster. Still being hunted as the remainder of the Dalton Gang, they became the nucleus of the vicious Wild Bunch led by Doolin.

THE WILD BUNCH RIDES 4

DOOLIN, NEWCOMB, AND PIERCE found temporary sanctuary among their Ingalls friends but soon moved to an open cave under a large overhang of rocks near the confluence of Deer Creek and the Cimarron, in the northwestern corner of the Creek Nation. Doolin had discovered the cave while trailing Bar X Bar cattle from Red Fork station on the Frisco railroad. He already had determined who should become part of the Wild Bunch, and from their headquarters "it would be easy to get in touch" with the men he sought.

The third week of October—virtually before the gunsmoke had settled in Coffeyville—the trio scouted west along the Cimarron. Pierce suffered an attack of the grippe and was left at Dave Fitzgerald's horse ranch on Cowboy Flat. Fitzgerald had homesteaded there in the Oklahoma opening on a creek that bore his name. He had been a close friend of the Halsell cowboys. Proceeding northwest through Logan County, Doolin and Newcomb picked up a small, dark complexioned, and black-mustached youth named Oliver "Ol" Yantis.

Yantis, another acquaintance from the Cowboy Flat days, now farmed cotton on the homestead of his widowed sister, Mrs. Hugh McGinn, three miles southeast of Orlando. The Daltons had used the McGinn claim as a resting place in their flight from the Wharton robbery in 1891. Ol's sister reportedly "grew sweet on Bitter Creek" and had "lied nobly" about her guests to inquiring deputy marshals. Tired of farming cotton and imbued with tales of the Dalton Gang's exploits, Yantis readily agreed to "fill in" on the plan that Doolin had in mind.

The trio continued up the Cimarron, through the Cherokee Outlet, and entered Kansas near Bluff Creek, in Comanche County. On the afternoon of November 1, masked and wielding Winchesters, they robbed the Ford County Bank at Spearville of all cash on hand and $1,697 in treasury notes and fled south.

A dozen Spearville citizens took off in pursuit. Ford County's sheriff, Chalkley M. "Chalk" Beeson, led a posse from Dodge City southeast down the Arkansas to intercept the bandits. Other posses started in the same direction. But their western ponies proved no match for the "highly bred" mounts of the outlaws. At midnight the trio passed through Clark County and at daybreak reached the Outlet, where they rested, divided the loot, and separated. Doolin and Newcomb headed for their Creek Nation hideout. Yantis returned to his sister's farm southeast of Orlando.

The Spearville bank offered a $450 reward, and Sheriff Beeson sent post card descriptions of the robbers and their mounts to every town and way station south from the Kansas border. The "small, dark complexioned, black-mustached" bandit riding a "line-backed dun" sparked the interest of Stillwater's city marshal, Thomas J. "Tom" Hueston, and his brother, Hamilton B. "Ham" Hueston, who helped him enforce local ordinances. The McGinn homestead being equidistant between Guthrie and Stillwater, Yantis often visited both cities and was well known to the Huestons. He also rode a dun pony with a dark mane and tail and a dark stripe along its back.

At the Huestons' request, Beeson sent a witness from Kansas to the McGinn farm, posing as a horse buyer. Yantis had no horses to sell but mentioned a couple of neighbors who might. The witness identified him as one of the Spearville bandits.

On the night of November 29, the Huestons, with Beeson

and a Stillwater constable, George Cox, proceeded to Orlando. They arrived at the McGinn place in a heavy fog before dawn and took positions between the house and barn where the outlaw kept his dun pony. At daybreak, Yantis emerged from the back door of the house with a feed bag under one arm. Beeson called on him to surrender. Yantis dropped the feed sack, snatched a pistol from a shoulder holster, and fired in the direction of the sheriff's voice. The posse responded with shotguns and rifles. Yantis fell, bleeding profusely. He was taken by wagon to the nearest doctor at Orlando, where he died in the afternoon, "making no confession or admission." In his heavy leather pocketbook was a portion of the bank's silver certificates.

The *Dodge City Globe* of December 2 lauded Sheriff Beeson alone for the killing of Yantis (the *Stillwater Gazette* credited Cox and City Marshal Hueston) and predicted that Yantis' confederates soon "will be behind bars or meet the fate of their comrade." The *Globe's* prophecy, however, would remain unfulfilled for some time to come.

In the national elections of November 8, the Democratic party candidate, Grover Cleveland, was returned for a second term as president of the United States. Cleveland was inaugurated March 4, 1893, and for months federal law enforcement in Oklahoma Territory was in political limbo. Disordered political conditions resulting from the elections on both local and territorial levels also took the bite out of law enforcement—much to the gratification of the Wild Bunch.

During the spring of 1893, President Cleveland made a "nearly clean sweep" of territorial Republican appointees. William C. Renfrow, a Norman banker and an ardent Cleveland supporter, became territorial governor. Frank Dale, a former Wichita, Kansas, attorney, succeeded Judge Green as chief justice and judge of the First Judicial District encompassing Payne and Logan counties; John H. Burford of Indiana was retained as judge of the Second Judicial District; and Henry W. Scott of Oklahoma City, another former Kansan, replaced John G. Clark in the Third Judicial District. Horace Speed, who had established himself as a fearless and incorruptible prosecutor, was retained as a

U.S. district attorney; and Evett Dumas Nix succeeded
William Grimes as U.S. marshal.

Nix, a native of Kentucky, was only thirty-two and the
youngest of twenty-three applicants. He had no law enforcement experience. His knowledge of the profession had
been gained from his father, S.S. Nix, who had served as
a lieutenant in the Confederate Army and was for several
years after the war a deputy sheriff in Calloway County,
at Murray. Young Nix had worked in a wagon and buggy
factory to complete his education, operated a grocery and
hardware business at Coldwater (which he sold at a good
profit in 1880), and served on the staff of the J.J. Bondurant
Company, wholesale grocers, at Paducah, Kentucky, before
coming to Oklahoma in 1889. At Guthrie, he entered the
general merchandise business with a man named Ed
Baldwin, purchased Baldwin's interest in March 1890, and
formed a wholesale grocery company with Oscar Halsell.
In 1891, when the Commercial Bank of Guthrie closed its
doors in the territory's first bank failure, Nix was appointed
receiver under bond of $450,000, and had disposed of the
institution's affairs so satisfactorily that he had become the
darling of the business community. Impressed with Nix's
executive ability, President Cleveland decided that he was
the man for the marshal's position.

In late May, Nix was in Washington to familiarize himself with the duties of his office prior to the effective date
of his appointment. He explained to Cleveland's new attorney general, Richard Olney, the hazards of transporting
merchandise and large amounts of money in the new country. He asked for 100 deputies—twice the number allowed
his predecessor. Olney advised him to commission only
a force of men adequate to solve the outlaw problem. Nix
bore no enmity for ex-Marshal Grimes' deputies—even
those who had questioned his qualifications—and asked
them to stay on until he could make satisfactory selections
for the various positions to be filled.

Meanwhile, Doolin added four new members to his Wild
Bunch—Tulsa Jack Blake (of his Oto reservation and 3-D
Ranch days), Dan "Dynamite Dick" Clifton, George "Red
Buck" Waightman, and Bill Dalton.

Clifton was a heavy-set, well-muscled man of fair intelligence—a cattle rustler and whiskey peddler from the Chickasaw Nation—and known as a "shrewd scouter and a dangerous criminal." He hollowed the leaden points of his rifle and revolver cartridges and filled them with dynamite to give them explosive as well as striking power, hence his alias.

Waightman was a horse thief and a killer—surly, vicious, stockily built, with heavy red mustache and auburn hair that gave him his nickname—and was known by every officer in Indian Territory. In 1890, he had been arrested for stealing some mules in the Cherokee Nation, convicted at Muskogee and sentenced to nine years in federal prison at Detroit. He escaped from a prison train as it left Lebanon, Missouri. Nothing more had been heard of him until he appeared at Ingalls with seven good (stolen) saddle horses that, Doolin acknowledged, the gang sorely needed.

Bill Dalton had brought his wife and two children to his mother's home at Kingfisher, to be at Emmett's bedside following the Coffeyville raid. Bitter and resentful over the pilfering of the personal effects of his brothers after they were gunned down, his failure to maintain any sort of damage suit against the city, and his own indictment as an alleged accomplice in the Alila train robbery, he "yearned to strike back at society" and sought out Doolin on the Cimarron. Doolin resented his presence; he visualized himself a greater bandit leader than Bob Dalton, and feared that Bill Dalton might jeopardize his control of the Wild Bunch. Dalton, however, convinced him that they should carry out their plans together.

At 1:20 A.M. on June 11, Doolin, Dalton, Newcomb, Dynamite Dick, and Tulsa Jack held up the Southern California-New Mexico Express on the Santa Fe a half-mile west of Cimarron, Kansas. They took $1,000 in silver from the way safe and fled toward the Outlet with the Gray County sheriff in hot pursuit. The trail led southeast past Ashland, in Clark County, across the Cimarron between Deep Hole and Snake creeks. The Kansas sheriff wired Sheriff Frank Healy at Beaver. Sheriff Healy hurried east with a posse and intercepted the gang above Fort Supply.

In a running gun battle, the bandits separated and escaped, but Healy managed to kill one of their horses and whang Doolin in the left foot with his .30–30 Winchester.

The wound was serious. Healy's steel-jacketed bullet had entered Doolin's heel and torn along the arch to the ball of his foot, shattering the bone. It gave the bandit leader such pain that he was forced to seek relief as soon as possible. He crossed the North Canadian west of Supply and rode south to a cow camp on Wolf Creek.

Old-time cowboy Billy McGinty supplied the rest of the story. Billy was working for the T.J. McElroy ranch south of Odessa, Texas, and had brought a herd of longhorns into the Outlet to pasture on the Box T range of the Dominion Cattle Company, pending their sale in Kansas City.

> Our pasture was on the Ivanhoe where it empties into Wolf Creek. The grass was knee high and there was plenty water, but lots of small canyons. . . bad country in which to hold mean, nervous steers. The night after Mac left for Kansas City a storm blew up. The whole herd stampeded. Next morning we had bawling cattle all over the hills. We made a circle into the northeast part of the Box T range and threw a roundup together. Then we separated our cattle from Box T stuff with little difficulty. But we were still about 500 short. I wanted to find as many lost steers as possible before Mac got back, so every day we would go through the range, finding a few more and driving them back at night.
>
> While working the Box T, I met another cowboy named Roy Daugherty. The night of the storm his herd of 2,800 longhorns from Tom Green County, Texas, had stampeded just south of us near the Fort Elliott-Camp Supply Trail, and his outfit was looking for strays bearing the Long H brand. He was tall and slender, with dark brown eyes and mustache, soft spoken, wore the best boots and Stetson, leather chaps and jacket, rode his horses hard, worked hard, and was young and full of devilment. The June sunshine warmed our backs, the Long H cook was a good one, which added to our well being, and we became good friends. He told me he had come from Arkansas and a family of preachers, had run away from home and a step-mother when he was four-

Roy Daugherty, alias "Arkansas Tom" Jones.

teen to become a cowboy and ended up with this Texas
outfit. We worked together about a week and caught 300
cattle belonging to our brands. . . .

One morning he told me a wounded man had come
to his camp during the night and was hiding in his tent.
The man's foot was so badly swollen Daugherty had to
cut his boot off to dress it. Some marshals came through
looking for robbers, but none of the boys had seen
anybody. I got a glimpse of Daugherty's guest later, at
a distance, and recognized Bill Doolin. . .but said
nothing. Doolin was in bad need of medical attention,
and Daugherty decided to take him on horseback to Ingalls, the closest place he could obtain a doctor he could
trust.

Billy saw Daugherty again about two months later:

McElroy had shipped his herd at Englewood, Kansas,
and I had gone to Ingalls to visit my father and register
for the opening of the Cherokee Outlet. . . .I moseyed
into Charley Vaughn's saloon and was surprised to see
Daugherty with Doolin and some others. When I called
him by name, he took me aside and told me he was now
"Arkansas Tom" Jones. Doolin must have paid him well
for the trip and filled him up with stories of easy money.
We took a ride out to Council Creek and sat down on
the bank and I tried to give him some advice. He told
me it was none of my business, and that I should never
mention the Daugherty name again.

Marshal Nix assumed his duties on July 1 and immediately named his office staff: John M. Hale, chief deputy; his father, S.S. Nix (who had joined him a few months
previous), chief clerk; W.S. Felts (an accountant in a local
bank), in charge of the financial department; and two
stenographers. Hale had been an Indian trader in the Osage
and on the Sac and Fox reservation, edited a Chandler
newspaper which supported the Democratic party, and had
many acquaintances and a thorough knowledge of the
country. During the week following, Nix appointed John
Hixon (former sheriff of Logan County), Christian "Chris"
Madsen (formerly Grimes' chief deputy), and Charles F.

Colcord (former sheriff of Oklahoma County) as district deputies for the First, Second, and Third judicial districts, with headquarters at Guthrie, El Reno, and Oklahoma City, respectively. He also commissioned twenty field deputies stationed at strategic points throughout the territory, retaining several Grimes men, including veteran gunfighters of the border Henry Andrew "Heck" Thomas and William Matthew "Bill" Tilghman.

The congressional act organizing Oklahoma Territory gave the U.S. marshal concurrent jurisdiction with county officers in criminal matters. Nix continued ex-Marshal Grimes' policy of deputizing eligible sheriffs, undersheriffs, city marshals, and Indian agency policemen at no extra cost to the government except the fees they earned but giving them authority to cross local boundaries in pursuit of felons. Those special deputies swelled Nix's force to nearly one hundred, which Doolin called a "little army." Among those eventually to engage the Wild Bunch in battle were James P. "Jim" Masterson, Logan County deputy sheriff; Richard "Dick" Speed, city marshal of Perkins; H.A. "Hi" Thompson, Payne County undersheriff; Tom Hueston (now constable) of Stillwater; and Lafayette A. "Lafe" Shadley, a deputy sheriff in Montgomery County, Kansas, at the time of the Dalton raid, now an Osage agency policeman at Pawhuska.

Before Nix could launch his campaign against the Doolin gang, he was shouldered with the responsibility of assisting the military in policing the opening of the eight-million-acre Cherokee Outlet, which President Cleveland, by proclamation of August 19, set for high noon on September 16. Five booths were set up in a hundred-foot-wide strip along the Kansas border and four along the southern border in Kingfisher, Logan, and Payne counties, where settlers filed their intentions and qualifications for homestead entry. Within the Outlet, four land offices were established and townsites set aside at Perry, a mile north of Wharton on the Santa Fe; at Enid, on the Rock Island; and at Alva and Woodward, on the Southern Kansas railroad.

The last week of August, Nix assigned most of his regular deputies along the northern borders of Kingfisher, Logan, and Payne counties where the majority of the hordes from Oklahoma Territory had assembled to await the opening. He sent Tilghman and Colcord to Perry and Chris Madsen to Enid to take charge of the townsites and land office crowds immediately upon the opening. One of the duties of the U.S. Marshal was to provide protection for the federal courts; Chief Deputy Hale was at Stillwater, where Judge Green was holding one of his last terms in the First Judicial District prior to being replaced by Cleveland's appointee, Frank Dale. Nix himself departed for Orlando, leaving Hixon and Heck Thomas at Guthrie to handle any emergencies.

On August 30, Hixon received word that the Doolin outlaws were rendezvoused at Ingalls, enjoying the fruits of the Cimarron train robbery.

THE
INVADERS 5

THERE ARE SEVERAL versions of how Marshal Nix's office learned that the Wild Bunch was making Ingalls headquarters.

One story goes that Doolin, upon reaching Ingalls, went to the O.K. Hotel, where his wound was treated by Mrs. Pierce; that Billy McGinty talked with him there but "did not know then when or how" he had been injured. Mrs. Pierce brought a pan of water and carbolic acid out on the porch to bathe the foot. Doolin could not bend over to reach the foot, it was so badly swollen, so Billy "came over to wash it." A deputy marshal was "looking for Doolin and passed close by." Doolin warned Billy to "get away," expecting the officer to draw on him, but the marshal walked on as if "oblivious of Doolin's presence" and notified Nix at Guthrie.

McGinty, however, never mentioned the incident in his many interviews with me. Actually, the hotel had no porch, there was no marshal in Ingalls, and Billy was still with the McElroy herd on Wolf Creek.

Edith Ellsworth was at the hotel. Since early June, she had been working for Mrs. Pierce, her "closest friend." The second week in March, just before her twentieth birthday, she had "gone north" to visit friends, but had secretly boarded a train to Kingfisher, where on March 14 she

became Mrs. William Doolin at the home of Adeline
Dalton. Doolin allegedly committed the Cimarron robbery
to obtain funds for their honeymoon. Edith had returned
to Ingalls and during April and May, carrying Doolin's
child, kept house for Mrs. Selph and helped in Doctor
Selph's office. Roy Daugherty brought Doolin to the hotel
the night of June 17. Mrs. Pierce summoned Doctor Selph.

The doctor recalled that he "removed many small par-
ticles of bone from Doolin's foot and advised him to give
it a rest." The women "wanted him to stay at the hotel"
where he could be "looked after," but the outlaw "could
not tarry." He asked Doctor Selph how much he owed him.
The doctor replied, "Whatever you think it's worth, Bill."
Doolin pointed to two sacks of silver on the table and said,
"Help yourself." The doctor told him, "I'll not do that,
Bill." Doolin then reached into his money belt and handed
him two twenty-dollar bills.

Meanwhile, Wells Fargo detective Fred Dodge interviewed the crew on the Southern California Express and
came away convinced that three of the robbers were Doolin,
Newcomb, and Tulsa Jack. The "language" and "expres-
sions" used by another member of the gang also "made
him know that Bill Dalton was there." He spent four days
in the Outlet and "got good identification" from some Indian scouts who had seen the gang "coming to, and coming from Cimarron." He contacted Sheriff Healy, "who was
sure the man he shot was Bill Doolin." Healy gave him
the shoes off the horse that had been killed.

Dodge knew the difficulty of obtaining information at
Ingalls, so he gave the shoes to "a friend who lived three
miles from town." The man went to Ingalls and obtained
"good information . . . the horse-shoer there was a good one
and verified his work." The animal had been one of four
brought to him by the outlaws a week before the robbery.

Dodge states in his autobiography, *Under Cover for Wells
Fargo*, that he was summoned to Texas on another case
that occupied him through August, but does not say
whether he shared his information with federal officers.

A third story extant is that a small-time thief named
"Ragged Bill" had beaten an old man in the head at

Stillwater and robbed him of forty dollars; that Robert N. "Bob" Andrews, a young deputy sheriff of Payne County, trailed him to Ingalls and found him in Ransom's saloon the night of June 17.

"Come peaceful, Bill," warned Andrews.

Ragged Bill ducked behind a gander-eyed, mustached man playing poker with four others at a nearby table. "Doolin," he cried, "I come to join your gang, don't let him arrest me!"

Andrews realized he was at the mercy of the Wild Bunch and retreated uneasily to the saloon entrance.

Doolin continued playing cards and said nothing. The only sounds in the room were the clicking of chips and the heavy breathing of the thief cowering behind him. Finally, he spread a winning hand and raked in the pot.

"What did this fellow do?" he asked Andrews.

Andrews told him, adding that his only reason for being in Ingalls was to take the man back to Stillwater.

Doolin whipped out his six-shooter. He ordered the culprit to hand his gun to the officer, and snorted, "Anybody who'd knock an old man in the head for forty bucks couldn't carry water for my outfit. Get the bastard out of here." He then told one of the men at the table, "Bitter Creek, get our horses. We'll ride a ways with the sheriff."

The two outlaws accompanied Andrews and his prisoner a short distance out of Ingalls. As they parted, Doolin said, "Sheriff, I'm taking your word that you won't tell anybody you saw me. If you do, we'll meet again sometime!"

Andrews thanked the bandit chief and proceeded to Stillwater. He never mentioned the Wild Bunch. Ragged Bill talked in jail, however, and details of his capture soon were known to the Guthrie marshals.

Andrews' alleged exploit first appeared in 1930 in Lon R. Stansbery's *The Passing of the 3-D Ranch*. It was embellished in his 1936 article, " 'Cops and Robbers' in Territorial Days," based on an interview with Orrington "Red" Lucas. A retired federal officer living near Wagoner, Oklahoma, Lucas claimed to have been an eyewitness. It has been accepted and cited by many writers since to show that these outlaws had hearts, even though they were thieves and hijackers.

Contemporary and official records mention no such robbery at Stillwater nor any person named Ragged Bill. Further, June 17 was the night Doolin arrived in Ingalls with a shattered foot (hardly in condition to be escorting a deputy out of town), and Lucas did not appear on the scene until several weeks later.

Payne County officials were aware of the Doolin gang's presence at Ingalls shortly after the Spearville robbery. Sterling Price King had become prosecuting attorney in the first territorial elections of 1892. In his unpublished autobiography, prepared before his death at St. Louis in 1947 and excerpted in *True West* as "More Rose of Cimarron" in 1955, King relates how his election placed upon him "the duty to get rid of the gang of outlaws. . . rendezvoused in the twelve miles east of Stillwater. . . that robbed banks and railroads, distributed their money freely among the citizens, and was menacing the security of the county. . . . They and the citizens were close friends. If any person in that locality was not a direct recipient of their favors he knew enough not to say anything against [them]."

King says Sheriff Frank M. Burdick of Payne County tried to deputize several citizens to help dispose of the gang, but all declined to serve. As one remarked, "he had not lost any outlaws and had no reason to go hunting for something he had not lost." So King went to Guthrie to enlist the aid of the United States marshal as "another method of reaching the nest of vipers." The marshal "flatly stated that it was contrary to the policy of the national government to participate. . . in purely local matters." King then approached U.S. District Attorney Horace Speed. "I explained to him that outlaws were running loose because our county did not have the money to finance a campaign of extermination. . . . Speed was favorably impressed and, as a result, President Benjamin Harrison ordered the United States marshal to assume the duty of arresting, dead or alive, every member [of the gang]." The movements of the outlaws were "followed closely as possible. . . . Some people were afraid to disclose their location, if they knew;

others knew but would protect them by giving false information to mislead the officers.'' After much ''fine detective work,'' the outlaws were ''disclosed at Ingalls.''

Constable Tom Hueston apparently knew of Detective Dodge's discovery or was testing the waters for County Attorney King. After being commissioned under Marshal Nix, he made his first trip as federal deputy to Ingalls on July 7, accompanied by a posseman named Wilson. The *Oklahoma State Capital* of July 10 reported:

> They rode into the town without thought of danger near. Just as they were dismounting they were covered by guns in the hands of Bill Dalton, Bill Doolin, Newcomb, and a man calling himself Starr [Tulsa Jack?], and told not to get off their horses but to move on. [The gang] having the drop on them, of course they had to submit, but have now organized a posse and are after the outlaws.
>
> The same gang were at Ingalls some time ago and had their horses shod at a blacksmith shop. They seem to have sympathizing friends at that place that the citizens [need to] look after.

The *Stillwater Gazette* commented that while the majority of Ingalls residents were ''God-fearing, law-abiding people,'' they were ''so terrorized by the gang'' that they kept silent. Many were ''in full sympathy with the outlaws, shielding them for the sake of getting their trade. . . . Whenever an effort is made to capture the gang, they generally have warning and are thus given a chance to escape into the unsettled reservations of the Pawnee and Creek Indians.''

By July, Doolin's foot had healed, attended by Doctor Selph, who met the bandit chief at night in various locations. When ready to make one of those calls, the doctor would ''put out all lights to appear that his family had retired,'' then slip away from the house on foot. He was not allowed to make the trips on horseback ''for fear he would be seen.'' The doctor did not wish to be seen, either, fearing that ''a raid might be made,'' and he ''did not care to be present upon such an occasion.'' Sometimes he would "crawl across a road to keep from being discovered."

Many stories have been told (and grown with each tell-ing) of how the free-spending Wild Bunch boosted the town's poor economy, enjoyed oyster stew socials given to raise funds for various projects, and contributed to the larders of indigent settlers during the summer of 1893. They are "remembered" as "soft-spoken, quiet fellows" who were "first to take off their Stetson when around women," and even attended church. On one divine occa-sion in a tent tabernacle near Main Street, a group of local yahoos became so obstreperous that the minister was unable to deliver his sermon. Doolin, carrying his Win-chester close to his leg and favoring his left foot, limped grimly down the aisle and muttered, "If you bastards don't shut up, I'm goin' to sift lead through some of you." The service proceeded "as demure and orderly as a Puritan Sun-day School."

Leamon Myers gave a different assessment of the gang's behavior:

> They drank and gambled in the two saloons. They'd play poker, then drink a while, throw a ten or a twenty dollar bill on the counter, and never ask for change. Bit-ter Creek was the happy one—always had fun throwing beer on the boys at the bar. . . .
>
> One time two of them came into Ransom's saloon and had a drink. One was reading a newspaper, leaning back in his chair. The other one was in a hurry to go some place. But the fellow just kept reading the paper, so the other one pulled his gun and starts shooting up the floor between his legs. You know, the one in the chair just sat there, didn't move or bat an eye.
>
> It was Charley Pierce did the shooting and it was the one known as Auger Eye [Red Buck] in the chair. He was the meanest of the bunch, and the most suspicious. He'd as soon shoot a man for nothing as not.

Sherm Sanders admitted that some of the gang were "cruel and treacherous." He had "herded cattle, cooked out on the range with Bill Doolin, Bitter Creek, and Tulsa Jack" when they were "real cowboys" and "fun to be with." When they "turned out [outside the law]," Sanders "couldn't go along with them."

Mrs. Addie C. Harp of Cushing, who worked at the O.K. Hotel, offered this perspective:

> Mr. & Mrs. Pierce, their girl and I slept upstairs right across from the outlaws. There was nothing but a curtain hung up but no one was afraid. I went to dances with all of them. . . . Maybe that is not saying too much for me but I was young and they behaved good. . . . Of course, they had it in for my husband's brother, who had been a marshal. He had a nice horse and saddle. He came to Ingalls once, and they took both. If they saw a horse they liked they just took it and left theirs. They didn't bother my dad because his "harness" [six-shooter and cartridge belt] was always hanging on the side of the house and we always let them alone.

Doctor Pickering's diary provides the best account of the gang's activities:

> In July Wm. Doolan, George Newcomb (alias) Bitter Creek [and] Slaughter Kid, Tom Jones (alias) Arkansas Tom, Danimite Dick, Tulsa Jack, and Bill Dalton began to come here frequently & in a short time they all stayed here except Dalton. He was at B Dunns. . . . They all went hevily armed & constantly on their guard, generly went 2 together. They boarded at the O.K. Hotel [and] staid at B Dunn's when not in town. . . .
>
> The last of the month a man by the name of Dock Roberts and Red Lucas came to town looking up a proposed Rail Road rout. Both parties took in the haunts of the outlaws. They were both jovial fellows & soon was drinking & playing cards with them. They left & came back in a week & said they were here to locate a booth, a place for intended settlers to register and get certificates to make the race for land or town lots [in the Outlet]. They stayed here until the last week in August then left.

Orrington Lucas was thirty-six, a native of Ohio, of Irish descent, and nicknamed "Red" because of the color of his drooping mustache and hair. He began his career as a detective with the Muncie, Indiana, police department, where he was noted for his "uncanny ability" to change disguise.

By 1882, he was riding as a deputy marshal for the Fort Smith federal court in the Cherokee and Creek nations. In 1889, he had obtained a couple of lots in Guthrie. He served under U.S. Marshal Grimes until recommissioned by Marshal Nix.

In his 1937 interview, Lucas stated that Ingalls was "so well known as an 'outlaw town' that even peace officers stayed away from it." On the eve of the Outlet opening, "it took on renewed activity." The outlaws had "won the good will of the people by setting themselves up as Robin Hoods. That is why officers received no cooperation in their single attacks on the gang. I planned to 'get in' with the outlaws, gain their confidence and at the opportune time have them surrounded and taken." Lucas chose as a partner Capt. W.C. "Doc" Roberts, another federal officer unknown to the Wild Bunch. Outfitted with good team and covered wagon, supplies, surveying instruments, and trailing saddle horses, they arrived at Ingalls late in July. "We pitched camp just south of the outlaws' [Ransom's] saloon. . . . The land south and west [which gullied off toward a tributary of Council Creek] was covered with weeds and brush and enclosed in a fence." The two men's operations during the next few weeks were essentially as described in Doctor Pickering's diary.

On August 30, Lucas and Roberts moved their "survey outfit" into a wooded ravine on the Council Creek tributary. Lucas remained at the camp to monitor the gang's activities. Roberts crossed the Cimarron and rode in the night thirty miles to Guthrie and delivered their final report to Deputy Marshal Hixon.

Hixon planned to enter Ingalls in two covered wagons, posing as homeseekers bound for the Outlet, "so not to attract attention." Heck Thomas declined to participate and called it a "fool's errand." In his nearly two decades of manhunting in Texas, Oklahoma Territory, and the Indian nations, he had seen too many such expeditions fail. He always had gone after his quarry alone or with no more than three possemen. Hixon, somewhat irritated, said, "I

Deputy U.S. Marshal Thomas J. Hueston, slain in Ingalls battle, September 1, 1893.

Deputy U.S. Marshal Lafayette "Lafe" Shadley, slain in Ingalls
battle, September 1, 1893.

reckon *one* of us ought to stay in Guthrie.''

Quietly, he organized a force of invaders. At nightfall on August 31, one wagon left Stillwater and another left Guthrie, each with a single driver. But carefully concealed beneath the canvas was a cargo of arms, ammunition, and thirteen federal officers. The Stillwater wagon, with Tom Hueston in charge, Dick Speed driving, and manned by Ham Hueston, Henry Keller, George Cox, M.A. Iauson, and Hi Thompson, reached Lucas' group shortly after eleven o'clock that night.

Hi Thompson, reminiscing on the invasion in June 1940, stated that Lucas had the Wild Bunch "located at the hotel...their horses in Ransom's livery stable.... We expected to surround the hotel at midnight and capture the desperados, but the Guthrie wagon was delayed and did not join us till daybreak." In this wagon rode Hixon, Jim Masterson (driver), Doc Roberts, Isaac A. "Ike" Steel, J.S. "Steve" Burke, and Lafe Shadley.

> This delay caused us to revise our plan.... Lucas went in to restudy the situation and returned at nine o'clock. He reported Doolin, Dalton, Newcomb, Dynamite Dick, and Tulsa Jack had gone to Ransom's saloon for their early-morning drinking and game of poker. Pierce, Waightman, and Arkansas Tom were "not on deck" and thought to have gone out to Bee Dunn's....
>
> While we were talking over the matter, one of our pickets caught a ragged youngster hiding in the brush, eyes and ears wide open. Lucas said he was one of the local boys who fished in the creek and was paid two-bits by the outlaws to warn them of any strangers. We questioned the boy, then chained him to a tree for later disposition.

Hixon, perhaps remembering Heck Thomas' warning, decided the odds of thirteen lawmen against five desperate criminals were not good enough. He sent Iauson to Stillwater with a message for Chief Deputy Hale. Hale, Sheriff Burdick, and O.W. Sollers, Stillwater's new city marshal, gathered eleven men "known to be good shots," and started for Ingalls at once.

Meanwhile, Hixon moved his forces to cut off all avenues of escape. The Guthrie wagon skirted eastward. "Hixon's original intention," said Thompson, "was to have his men get out at some haystacks at the corner of town, but to have an unobstructed view of most of the settlement, drove up Oak Street into a grove of trees north of the Pickering home." Speed drove his wagon north, thence east on First Street, or Section Line Road. As he approached the town limits, the Huestons, Keller, Cox, and Hi Thompson dropped from under the canvas and scattered south behind the brush, buildings, and fences between Walnut and Ash streets. At Ash Street, Speed turned his empty vehicle south past Light's blacksmith shop, closely followed by Lucas' "survey outfit," and stopped in front of the Pierce-Hostetter stable.

Witness Doctor Pickering's diary:

> [The] marshals piloted into town in covered waggons. They caused no suspicion as there was hundreds of Boomers moving the same way. 2 waggons stoped at Light's Black Smith Shop & one drove up by my house & they all proceeded to unload in a quite man-ner. . . . Doolan, Bitter Creek, Danimite Dick, Tulsa Jack & Dalton were in Ransoms & Murrys Saloon. Arkansas Tom was in bed at Hotel.

INGALLS UNDER SIEGE 6

DOWN THE YEARS A NUMBER of Ingalls residents remembered what they were about that clear fall morning of Friday, September 1, 1893. A warm sun had dispelled the fog from the valleys. A brisk breeze from over the Cimarron rustled the trees that dotted the square. Charley Vaughn opened his front and back doors, taking advantage of the morning coolness to air out his saloon. Joe Ketchum walked over to Sherm Sanders' barber shop to show him a new relic he was going to exhibit.

The breakfast hour at the hotel over, Mary Pierce was with her two children in the dining room, churning butter. Mrs. Call was sweeping her porch next door. Across the street Mrs. Wagner was hanging over her front fence, discussing plans for an upcoming basket-social with Mrs. Bill Wilson, who had dropped by en route to Perry's dry goods to look at some new dress material.

Five-year-old Ernest and seven-year-old Harry Selph were shooting marbles in the street in front of their father's grocery. I interviewed the brothers and walked the Ingalls townsite with Ernest many times during 1954–1955.

Ernest recalled that Doctor Selph had just amputated a finger for Lew Ferguson, who "got it smashed in a threshing machine accident" and was in the store with Lew "getting something to ease his pain." Dent Ramsey stepped

73

over from his implement yard "to see how Lew was
doing." Arkansas Tom had passed the boys in the street.
"He wasn't feeling well and was on his way back to the
hotel. He stopped and gave Harry and me two sticks of
gum....He was always giving us gum. We called him
'Chewing Gum' Tom."

Minutes before, Bitter Creek Newcomb had taken his
horse to Wagner's blacksmith shop to have a shoe tight-
ened. Harry remembered, "He called the horse 'Old
Ben'—a big sorrel, very fleet of foot. Bitter Creek valued
him highly because of his endurance. Old Ben belonged
to George Ransom later, but like Bitter Creek, met an
unhappy end. About 1902 some fellow borrowed him to
go hunting...in shooting at a rabbit the fellow aimed
wrong and shot the horse through the head."

Newcomb had returned to Ransom's saloon and was
leaning against the end of the bar inside the doorway, eye-
ing Sadie Comley's establishment, which he patronized
often, and watching his companions—Doolin, Dalton,
Dynamite Dick, and Tulsa Jack—play poker. At the far end
of the bar, old Si Newlin, the town drunk, was well into
his cups. The only other bar customer at this early hour
was N.A. Walker, a hotel supply salesman from Cushing.

Newcomb saw the covered wagon stop in Pickering's
grove. That was a favorite camping place for travelers, so
he thought nothing of it. When the other wagons stopped
in front of the livery stable, he decided to investigate. He
crossed to Wagner's to see if his mount was ready.

In the meantime, Bob Beal had gone out to check his
ponies in Querry's pasture and met five men in a covered
wagon on the Main Street road. The driver, Dick Speed,
asked if there was a good place to eat in Ingalls. Beal told
him there was a restaurant, and they could also get
something at the hotel. They "posed as hunters," but had
"all the appearances of lawmen and were heavily armed."
As the wagon proceeded northward, Beal conveyed his
suspicions to Mr. Querry, then "slipped back into town"
and told Sherm Sanders. "Sherm said we ought to spread
the alarm."

It was too late to warn anybody, however. Dick Speed

H.F. Pierce livery stable in Ingalls at the time of the famous battle, September 1, 1893.

had climbed down from his wagon and entered the open door of the livery barn, covering its only two occupants with his Winchester. Present were Henry Pierce and his twelve-year-old stable boy, Oscar Wagner. Pierce testified afterwards, "He told us he was a federal officer...that there was going to be some shooting, and if either of us tried to notify the outlaws, we'd be killed like dogs."

The statements of Red Lucas and Hi Thompson; testimony given later in Territory of Oklahoma vs. Tom Jones (Case No 323, District Court of Payne County); Marshal Nix's report to Attorney General Richard Olney (Records of United States Marshal for Oklahoma Territory, Guthrie, 1893–1895); and contemporary accounts in the *Stillwater Gazette, Perkins Journal, Oklahoma State Capital,* and *Guthrie Daily Leader* provide the details.

As Speed stepped back to the doorway of the livery barn, Newcomb left Wagner's and started walking his horse up Ash Street toward the marshal's wagon. At that moment, fourteen-year-old Del Simmons left Light's blacksmith shop. Speed called him to the doorway and inquired, "Who is that rider?" The youth, incredulous that anyone did not know Newcomb, exclaimed, "Why, that's Bitter Creek!" Newcomb heard, saw the boy point his direction, and jerked his rifle from its scabbard. Speed threw his Winchester to his shoulder and fired the opening shot in the most deadly affair of its kind in the lawless West.

Speed's bullet "burst the magazine" of Bitter Creek's weapon and ricocheted into his upper right leg and groin. The outlaw flinched in pain, and his shot missed the marshal. Unable to lever for a second shot, he wheeled Old Ben for a getaway. Speed stepped clear of the doorway to kill him.

The rifle blasts brought Arkansas Tom from his bed on the upper floor of the hotel. Snatching up his Winchester, he sprang to the north gable window, saw the situation at a glance, and fired at Speed, hitting him in the shoulder. Speed started back to the stable door, then tried to reach the shelter of his wagon. Arkansas Tom fired again, and the marshal fell, a bullet in his chest and coughing his life's blood.

The firing precipitated a battle before the other officers had reached their assigned positions. Hixon's men in Pickering's grove began shooting at Newcomb as he dashed wildly down Ash Street, barely able to stay in the saddle and still gripping his disabled weapon. Doolin, Dalton, Dynamite Dick, and Tulsa Jack opened fire from Ransom's saloon to help him escape. At the creek south of town Newcomb met a family en route to Ingalls and paused long enough to shout, "Tell my pals I can do them no good— I'm bad hurt and have only a farmer's gun"—which meant that he could load his rifle with only one cartridge at a time.

Del Simmons had caught Bitter Creek's first movement in the street and darted into Vaughn's saloon. He ran through the building, came out the back door, and was struck down by a bullet. He died at 6:00 P.M. Doolin sympathizers maintained that the youth had been slain in the barrage from Pickering's grove. Contemporary accounts and testimony in Territory vs. Jones, however, confirm that Arkansas Tom was "in direct range from the north window of the hotel . . . the only man in position to have killed him, mistaking him for a marshal."

When Newcomb disappeared, Hixon's men concentrated their fire on the saloon. Neil Murray's horse, hitched at the rail and standing broadside of the building, interfered with their aim at the front door and was "killed intentionally." A chicken crossing the street was "knocked into the air" by stray lead; it squawked a couple of times, fell to the ground, and lay motionless. N.A. Walker ran into the street and was "shot through the liver by marshals thinking he was one of the outlaws trying to escape."

Inside the saloon, Leamon Myers took refuge in a big ice box where the liquor was stored. "It sounded like a hail storm when the marshals turned loose on the place. The sawdust in that ice box saved my life," he said. Si Newlin, passed-out on the floor at the end of the bar, also went unscathed.

Havoc reigned as the populace sought cover. Several "took to a corn field" between Main and Walnut streets and "lay flat between the ridges." Mary Pierce ushered her children into the cellar at the rear of the hotel. A drummer named Van Horn, who had just driven up in front of the place, wheeled his buggy between the hotel and Doctor Call's home and beat a hasty retreat up Oak Street and east along Section Line Road.

The Selph boys forgot to pick up their marbles. "We had always been told by father to go to our cave when we heard gunfire," Ernest said, "and that's where we ran." Harry added, "We jumped a fence more than three feet high west of Ransom's house and went into the cave feet first."

Inside the grocery, Ferguson and Dent Ramsey ducked behind three empty barrels sitting in the middle of the floor. Doctor Selph—"to have some fun"—kicked the barrels over and the two men scurried from the rear of the store into a gully a hundred yards away. Fearing for the safety of his wife and child, the doctor then left the front door and strode briskly up the street to his home. "The outlaws knew me—so did the marshals—and I had little fear of being shot," he said. "Some bullets had hit the house, and my wife had put the baby on the floor under a feather bed. I took them to the [Selph] cave [already overflowing with women and children, shouting and crying], and waited for a lull in the fighting before going back into the street to tend the wounded."

Mrs. Wagner likewise braved the flying lead and ran to her husband's blacksmith shop. She insisted that he return to their home, but decided to "set out the battle" with him behind a pile of scrap iron in the rear of the shop.

Meanwhile Tom Hueston led his men behind the buildings on the west side of Ash Street to cover the rear of the saloon. Hixon's men advanced from Pickering's grove along both sides of Second, sheltered by the hotel and homes of McMurtry, Selph and Call, to better cover the front of the saloon and livery stable where the outlaws had left their horses. After the first burst of firing, Hixon shouted to Doolin, "You are surrounded—surrender!"

Doolin replied, with an oath, "Go to hell!"

The marshals poured a withering barrage into the saloon—front, north side, and rear. "There were 172 bullet holes in that building when it was over," Myers claimed. "Ransom was hit in the leg . . . he became my guest in the

Ransom and Murray Saloon, Ingalls, O.T.

ice box. It got so hot in the saloon that the boys [outlaws] had no choice but to break for their horses.

Doolin went first, followed quickly by Dalton, Dynamite Dick, and Tulsa Jack. The Nix-Olney report says they escaped through a half-finished shed on the south side of the saloon where Ransom kept a pool table, and the marshals "did not know the building was deserted until they were fired upon from the stable." For distraction, Murray "appeared in the doorway [of the saloon]. . . Winchester to his shoulder in the act of firing. Three of the deputies seeing him in the position. . . fired at him simultaneously. Two shots struck him in the ribs and one broke his arm. . . . He pitched forward into the street, his Winchester falling across the threshold."

The "bold dash" by the outlaws forced Hueston and his men to change positions. Hueston darted behind a small pile of lumber at the corner of the granary between Perry's dry-goods and Doctor Briggs' residence, where he could command the rear of the stable. According to testimony in Territory vs. Jones, the deputy was "facing south, directly west from the hotel, but in easy range. . . . He could not be seen from the upstairs [gable windows]. However, the shingles of the roof were punched off from inside [by Arkansas Tom] and a hole sufficiently large made. . . directly in view of Hueston." Arkansas Tom "mounted a chair, or some other article of furniture giving him height enough to shoot downward through the hole [and] shot the deputy in the left side and bowels."

Ham Hueston, Cox, Keller, and Thompson hunkered behind Doctor Briggs' home, disconcerted and trying to determine the source of the sniper lead. Dalton and Tulsa Jack, pumping a close, accurate fire from the livery stable, slowed Hixon's men while Doolin and Dynamite Dick saddled the horses.

Hixon took cover in a shallow ditch in front of Pickering's home and pumped shot after shot into the stable doorway. Masterson stood nearby behind a blackjack tree "little more than half as thick as his body," with outlaw lead barking its trunk, cutting off limbs, and "tearing holes in the ground all about him." Nonetheless, the valiant brother of the famed Bat Masterson of the Kansas trail-town days "stood his ground until his ammunition was exhausted," then raced back to the wagon in Pickering's grove for "a fresh supply of cartridges."

At that point, the four outlaws burst from the stable—Dalton and Tulsa Jack from the front door, Doolin and Dynamite Dick from the rear—"riding hell-bent south and west toward a draw."

As Dalton galloped from the barn, Hixon shot his horse in the jaw. The animal stopped. Dalton put the spurs to him. The horse spun around and became "almost unmanageable."

Doctor Pickering writes that Dalton "had a hard time getting him started but finally succeeded. He went probely 75 yards when his horse got his leg broke."

Lafe Shadley, firing from behind Doctor Call's house, hit the horse in the leg.

"As they went down," Thompson said, "Dalton jumped clear on the opposite side of the horse. Shadley fired again, and thought he had killed him and started toward the other outlaws who had stopped at the wire fence, when Dalton reappeared and ran back to his injured horse. The gang's only pair of wire cutters were in his saddlebags."

It has been claimed that Dalton saw Shadley running toward him and shot him three times, the wounds being so close together they could be covered with one hand. On the contrary the *Capital* and *Gazette* reported, "Shadley was south and west of Call's house in direct range from the south gable windows of the hotel. . . . In trying to get through Ransom's fence his coat caught, throwing him forward. . . . While in this position . . . a shot was fired from the upper chamber of the hotel. . . . The ball struck him in the right hip, shattering the bone, and lodged in his right breast. . . . He freed himself and went to Ransom's house. Mrs. Ransom refused him admittance, telling him to go to Selph's cave."

Doctor Pickering agrees, "He got to Ransom's house & was debating with Mrs. Ransom she ordering him to leave. . . . He fell there & crawled to Selph's cave. A great many say he [Dalton] shot him. In fact Shadly thought so

for when I & Dr. Selph was working with him in the cave
he said Dalton Shot him...but I think I know better....I
stood where I saw Dalton most of the time & never saw him
fire once & Shadly was hit in the right hip and [the ball]
tended downward. If Dalton had of Shot him he would of
been Shot in front & ball ranged up[ward]."

Shadley's plight gave Dalton time to cut the fence and
let the gang ride into the draw. Masterson described the
ensuing action in a November 15 interview. "This gully
was about ten feet deep....I didn't know it till I saw their
hats....They came out of the gully on the jump. Dalton
was up behind Doolin....'Hell,' says I, 'fellers, they're
getting away.' Well, we blazed away at 'em and Dalton
tumbled off [the horse]. They stopped, lifted him in the
saddle, and Doolin got up behind. I raised my sight to 500
yards, but I couldn't get 'em."

Masterson afterwards learned that the wounded outlaw
was Dynamite Dick, not Dalton. The bullet later was
removed from Dynamite Dick's neck, leaving an obvious
scar that would help marshals identify him.

Doctor Briggs' urchin son, Frank, was "so intensely in-
terested in the fight" that he stood near Thompson, Keller,
and Cox, "watching the effects of their broadsides" as the
outlaws fled to the draw. He then dashed to the intersection in front of Pickering's home "to see which way they
went." The outlaws topped a slope southeast of town and
paused, firing back along Oak Street, and one of their shots
struck young Briggs.

Doctor Pickering describes the incident:

> The outlaws [were] shooting up the street my house
> is on. One of these shots hit Frank Briggs in the Shoulder
> but a slight flesh wound. I took him to cave & dressed
> the wound then went to Walker & gave him Tempory
> aid [Walker died two weeks later] from there to Murry's
> & Laid his wound open & removed the shattered bone.
> Some of the Drs. wanted me to Amputate but I fought
> for his arm. 2 inches of radius was shot away slight flesh
> wounds in the side. About this time I was called aside
> & told to go to Hotel that Jones [Arkansas Tom] was up
> there either wounded or killed.

O.K. Hotel, Ingalls, O.T., 1893.

The outlaws fled southeast from the hill toward Falls City, but the marshals held their positions. It was apparent that Shadley had not been hit by the firing from the livery stable, and Hueston could not have been seen from the saloon. Thompson said:

> The bullet that downed Hueston had passed between two buildings from the east [the restaurant and Perry's dry goods.] In tracing its direction, we discovered a hole in the roof of the hotel. Then a woman told Hixon that she had seen puffs of smoke rise from the roof and the gable windows.
>
> We surrounded the building, but Mrs. Pierce said none of the outlaws was there. The woman who had talked to Hixon boldly walked upstairs, saw Arkansas Tom Jones, and told us Mrs. Pierce had lied...that the outlaw knew he would be taken but not until he'd killed some more marshals. Hixon ordered everyone out of the building, and all left except Jones. He knocked a hole in the east roof to have a view of the town in every direction.
>
> We opened fire on the hotel, but all were shooting upward through the gables and both sides of the roof and the outlaw had only to lay on the floor to survive. At 11 o'clock, he was still shooting down at us and seemed to have plenty of ammunition.

The Stillwater reinforcements arrived. Chief Deputy Hale led the posse in pursuit of the Wild Bunch. Sheriff Burdick and City Marshal Sollers joined the siege at the hotel. "The sheriff and I identified ourselves to Jones," Sollers remembered. "We asked him to surrender, and he hollered back: 'If I come out, I'll come out shootin'!'"

At that juncture, the marshals allegedly decided to burn him out. Several latter-day writers claim that one of them "piled kindling wood" against the hotel; others say they piled hay on the running gears of a wagon to be pushed against the building. As they were about to light the fire, Jones "gave up...came down stairs calmly rolling a cigaret, and seemed to be the coolest man in the crowd."

Another version is that Masterson placed two sticks of dynamite beneath the east side of the building and told

Mrs. Pierce to bring Jones out or he would blow the place "into the middle of next week." Mrs. Pierce pleaded with him to spare the hotel as her "only means of livelihood." She called out to Jones, went upstairs, and within a few minutes "threw his rifle and six-shooters out the window and led him, bleeding from bullet wounds, down to the marshals." For a touching denouement, the outlaw tells Mrs. Pierce, "I would never have allowed your place to be destroyed." And the woman sheds crocodile tears, making Jones feel that he is a hero.

Neither incident occurred. There is some basis for the Masterson tale, however. Thompson admitted, "Masterson was hot for revenge over the shooting of Shadley, but none of us dared venture near the hotel and we had no dynamite. Masterson said if he could get some at the hardware store he would blow the place plumb to hell and Jones with it. . . . Hixon nixed the idea."

Doctor Pickering tells how the capture finally was made:

> I and Alva Pierce & a boy by name of Wendell boys about 12 years old went over. I went in & called out but got no answer and was about to leave when he [Jones] came to top of stairs & says is that you Dock & I told him it was. I asked if he was hurt & he said no. He said for me to come up & I told him if he wasent hurt I would not but he insisted. So I went up. He had his coat & vest off also his boots had his Winchester in his hands & revolvers lying on the bed. I said Tom come down and Surender. He says I cant do it for I wont get justice. He says I dont want to hurt anyone but I wont be taken alive. He says where is the boys (meaning the outlaws) I told him they had gone. He said he did not think they would leave him it hurt him bad I never seen a man wilt so in my life. He staid in Hotel till after 2 o'clock & then Surendered to a Mr. Mason, a preacher."

Jones was taken into custody by Sheriff Burdick and Red Lucas, who had "played poker with the gang as a good fellow." The outlaw looked at Lucas with surprise, and said, "Oh, so you're a United States man."

Hixon and another deputy climbed the stairs and

gathered up Arkansas Tom's weapons. The room had been "literally shot to pieces." Bullets had shattered a water pitcher, mirror, and "pierced everything else in the place." It "seemed a miracle" that the outlaw had not been killed or wounded.

The departure of Hale's posse from Stillwater had aroused more than curiosity. When word of the battle was received, Judge Green "found it necessary to adjourn court"; the town was "virtually emptied of citizens, witnesses, jurors and lawyers rushing to the scene of carnage." Additional searching parties spread through the timbered hills and ravines toward Council Creek and the Cimarron. The Guthrie *Leader* observed: "Another battle may be looked for, and if it comes. . . from the temper of the people. . . it will be a war of extermination."

Arkansas Tom viewed the Stillwater arrivals with apprehension. He demanded protection and asked Sheriff Burdick not to place him in chains.

"The sheriff asked whether I could get the prisoner to Stillwater safely," Sollers said, "and I replied that I could if I wasn't ambushed by his friends on the way. We put Jones on the seat of a spring wagon, Iauson driving, Thompson and Cox behind with loaded guns. I followed in a buggy. Jones was not handcuffed, but when we were ready to start, I told the guards, 'Boys, don't let him get away under any circumstance,' and Jones gave me a look that would have put fear in the devil."

The body of Dick Speed and the wounded Hueston and Shadley were placed in one of the marshals' wagons, driven by Keller, and the grim cortege set off across the open country. By midafternoon, Jones was in the Payne County jail.

There are people who find humor in the most serious situation. Billy McGinty was one of them. Billy wasn't present during the fight. "I was west of town looking at some horses father had talked about buying," he said, "and got back after the gunsmoke had cleared." Arkansas Tom was en route to Stillwater. Folks had begun assessing the damage to their stores and homes.

Some of us were counting the bullet holes in Ransom's saloon and found old Newlin still there. He'd crawled behind the bar, propped himself against the wall, and was asleep. I thought what a joke it would be to remove the intestines from the dead chicken in the street and poke them down the bib of his overalls. We waited a while for his reaction, but he slept on, so we woke him up...told him there had been a big gun battle and that the saloon was full of bullet holes.

He blinked a few times, and we helped him to his feet. Then he saw the bloody entrails in his bib.... Well, he just grabbed his belly with both hands and ran out in the street, yelling, "My God, they've shot my guts out!"

I don't remember that he ever took another drink.

Deputy Hale's posse tracked the Wild Bunch to the Cimarron crossing at VanArsdale's logging camp, but lost them in the Sac and Fox country. They found bloodstains in a cornfield on the creek south of Ingalls where Newcomb had rested briefly; at Falls City, J.D. Vickrey admitted that the outlaw had ridden to his blacksmith shop, demanding a bucket of water. "He looked very pale," the *Capital* reported. "He wanted Vickrey to pour the water on his leg, which he did.... Vickrey asked him how it came that the wound wasn't bleeding and he remarked that he got off at the creek and washed it and succeeded in stopping the blood." He had "gone east at a fast trot."

Hale believed Newcomb had rejoined the Wild Bunch before they crossed the river, but it was soon rumored that the outlaws had hidden in the attic of Sherm Sanders' log house. The *Gazette* intimated knowledge of the matter: "One or maybe two [of the outlaws] are either fatally wounded or already dead. Bitter Creek...is known to have been shot through the hips...the last word of him...he was not able to be moved and his death was hourly expected."

Doctor Pickering writes in his diary:

All the outlaws staid close to town as Bitter Creek was not able to travel. Dr. Bland of Cushion [Cushing] tended him. I loaned him instruments to work on wound with,

although I did not know just where he was at. A piece
of magazine...blown in his leg...eventually worked
out and he got able to again ride.

The manhunt produced no results, and the *Leader*
lamented, "The farmers in that country, through fear or
sympathy, would keep sending the officers in the wrong
direction. The general opinion prevails that the bandits
have sought refuge in the Creek Nation."

The *Capital* added, "It is no easy thing to capture five
men, outlawed and having a lot of citizens protecting them
[but] the marshals were victorious, driving back their op-
ponents, capturing a town and making a number of ar-
rests."

Late in the evening, Hixon and Sheriff Burdick arrived
at Stillwater with Lon Case (the youngster left chained to
the tree by the marshals), his brother Al, and another boy
named Perrin. Deputies Masterson, Steel, Burke, and
Roberts, reached Guthrie with George Ransom, Sherm
Sanders, and the wounded Murray in custody, leading
Arkansas Tom's horse (left in Ransom's stable by the
outlaws) and carrying Bill Dalton's saddle. Ransom, Murray, and Sanders were held for harboring; the boys at
Stillwater were detained as witnesses. All were released
after questioning, however, and immediately returned to
Ingalls.

Marshal Nix explained in his report to Attorney General
Olney, "Ransom, Murray and other[s] catered to the
outlaws, carried them news of the movements of the deputy
marshals, furnished them with ammunition, cared for their
horses, permitted them to eat at their tables and sleep in
their beds. These facts were well known...although a conviction on the charge of harboring or aiding and abetting
criminals against the laws of the United States could never
be sustained, by reason...that the entire community was
under duress and would not testify for fear of losing their
lives and property."

News that Dick Speed had been "killed outright" in the
raid incensed Perkins citizens. Rumors that they intended
to give Arkansas Tom a "necktie party" became so rife by

nightfall that he was transferred to the federal jail at Guthrie.

Saturday afternoon, September 2, relatives and friends packed the Methodist Episcopal Church at Stillwater where Dick Speed's funeral was conducted by the Association of United Workmen Lodge No. 5, of which he was a "valued member." Some 300 persons attended the last rites at the Perkins cemetery, and editor Will G. Hill of the *Perkins Journal* paid him this tribute: "Richard Speed was but 26 years of age at the time of his death...of stainless character...respected by the law-abiding and feared by lawbreakers....He had the kindest of dispositions, was a devoted husband and father and a friend of sterling worth....He leaves a wife and three children."

Tom Hueston died the same afternoon at four o'clock. He, too, was a member of the AOUW Lodge No. 5 and a member of the International Order of Odd Fellows, holding the position of Noble Grand. The two lodges combined for his services on Sunday at the Methodist Church. Some 1,500 persons attended and followed his remains to the cemetery.

Lafe Shadley died on Sunday afternoon, and his remains were taken to his home at Independence, Kansas.

The *Stillwater Gazette* called Speed, Hueston, and Shadley "three as brave and fearless officers as ever operated in support of law and order...cut down in the prime of life by assassins while in defense of our homes and firesides. They are no more, but...their labors and deaths will form a page in the history of Oklahoma which will shine all the brighter and read the better when outlawry and organized bands of marauders are completely wiped out of existence."

The Guthrie *Leader* declared, "It is time that false glamor surrounding [the Doolin gang's] dastardly deeds be dispelled....Nothing will do this but the killing of the scoundrels as one kills a wild beast."

Marshal Nix's force vowed to accomplish just that.

On September 8, Deputies Hixon, Sam Bartell, Ed Clump, and Jim Masterson, searched the "wild and unsettled" confluence of Kingfisher Creek and the Cimarron near

Adeline Dalton's home, "having heard that Bill Dalton was hiding there." Dalton was not found, but despite the denials of his wife and aged mother, the officers remained in the vicinity until convinced that he had fled.

Shortly after eleven o'clock that night, Payne County jailer Turney Jackson was awakened by several men demanding to see Arkansas Tom. "They had gotten in through the gate of the outer fence and were hammering on the iron grating of the jail proper." Jackson thought they were sympathizers bent on rescuing the outlaw. Informed that he had been moved to Guthrie, they "swore around for awhile and on leaving bombarded the entrance way to the jail with heavy stones."

On September 11, much of Guthrie's population having departed for the opening of the Outlet, a startling rumor swept the city. Two men, their names "suppressed for obvious reasons," came in from Ingalls and reported the Doolin gang "rendezvoused five miles from the town...gathering reinforcements every day"; that they intended to raid Guthrie, "partly for pure cussedness, partly for revenge," and to liberate Arkansas Tom.

Deputy Heck Thomas discounted the proposed raid as "a big bluff"; nevertheless, he warned Guthrie officers and citizens to "keep their optics peeled."

Then Col. Dick Reaves of the cavalry unit at Guthrie reported "a formidable looking body of men," with "good horses and armed to the teeth," encamped twenty-two miles northeast of the city. Guns and ammunition were plentiful in Guthrie. Reaves announced that anyone could have a Winchester by applying to his department. Scores of citizens armed themselves, promising a repetition of the Coffeyville disaster. Thomas and Hixon, with two armed squads, hurried to the encampment, but the "suspicious looking gang" had vanished.

Guthrie was guarded three days and three nights. Nothing happened. At the federal jail, Arkansas Tom "guffawed loudly," credited the scare to Ingalls pranksters, and added, "Why, Bill and his boys ain't damn fools enough to try such a thing. Fust, Bill ain't even to it an' two are wounded. You fellows here are damned fools."

And Guthrie began to believe it.

Doctor Pickering concludes his account of the Ingalls battle:

> Dalton drifted away from the crowd.... The rest staid around the Dunns. Danimite ordered a big [50 caliber Sharps] gun sent to Tulsa. The marshalls got onto it & watched for him thinking he would come in at night to get it but he rode in at 2:00 P.M. & got his gun & was getting out of town before they knew it. They started after him & had a running fight from there to Turkey Track ranch. They killed 2 horses from under him. They thought they had him surrounded in the timber there & sent for more help but when they got it & searched through he was gone.... Bitter Creek and Tulsa [Jack] still staid here. Doolan disappeared and no one knew where, also Edith Elsworth. They probely went off together.

Chief Justice Frank Dale, First Judicial District, Oklahoma Territory, Guthrie.

"BRING THEM IN DEAD!" 7

On SEPTEMBER 16—IN THE grandest, wildest, and most colorful of all land rushes—the Cherokee Outlet, with the surplus lands of the Tonkawa and Pawnee reservations, was added to Oklahoma Territory, its population increased by 100,000, and the bloody battle at Ingalls and exploits of the Wild Bunch faded from newspaper headlines.

Seven new counties were organized and subsequently named Kay, Grant, Woods, Woodward, Garfield, Noble, and Pawnee, with seats at Newkirk, Medford, Alva, Woodward, Enid, Perry, and Pawnee, respectively. Payne County got its promised tier of townships—Rock, Walnut, Eden, Glencoe, and Rose—above its northern boundary, which put Stillwater in the exact center and for all practical purposes ended the county seat controversy. Later, Rock and Walnut townships were lost to Noble County to give Perry a more central location in its county seat fight. In compensation, Payne County's eastern boundary was extended to include that portion of the Pawnee reservation east of Ingalls and north of the Cimarron to the Creek Nation border.

To facilitate the handling of federal matters in the Outlet, Congress (by act approved December 21, 1893) added two territorial justices, thus increasing the membership of the supreme court and number of judicial districts to five. On February 3, 1894, Oklahoma Territory was redistricted by the supreme court as follows: First Judicial District, embracing Payne, Logan, Lincoln, and Pawnee counties, Judge Frank Dale presiding; Second Judicial District, embracing Canadian, Kingfisher, Blaine, Washita, and Garfield counties, Judge John R. Burford presiding; Third Judicial District, embracing Oklahoma, Cleveland, and Pottawatomie counties, Judge Henry W. Scott presiding; Fourth Judicial District, embracing Noble, Kay, Grant, and Woods counties, Judge Andrew G.C. Bierer presiding; Fifth Judicial District, embracing Woodward, Dewey, Custer, Day, Roger Mills, and Beaver counties, Judge John L. McAtee presiding. The northern half of the Osage reservation was attached to Kay County, the southern portion to Pawnee County, and the Ponca and Oto-Missouri reservations were attached to Noble County for judicial purposes.

Again, Marshal Nix had jurisdiction in the new counties only in federal offenses, such as cutting timber on government land, violations of revenue and postal regulations, and selling whiskey to Indians. For robbery, stock-thievery, and murder, his jurisdiction lay only in the Osage, the Wichita, Kiowa-Comanche-Apache, and other Indian reservations yet to be ceded for settlement. Federal marshals received no compensation for tracking down bank and train bandits. However, Nix assured the sheriffs of the new counties he would provide all possible assistance and continued his policy of deputizing qualified local officers.

The Wild Bunch also continued its policy of robbing banks and railroads.

By mid-October, the gang had again congregated in its Ingalls haunts. Charley Pierce "got a Pawnee Indian drunk and stole six of his ponies." Several good citizens of Ingalls received threatening letters "telling them that they took sides with the deputy marshals and had better pull their freight or it would be pulled for them." Doolin and Dalton "gave it out plainly" that they intended to kill Lucas and Doc Roberts "because they played the spies on the gang that led to the attack." On October 23, the Wild Bunch "capped the Ingalls battle when all appeared in Cushing at an oyster supper given by the ladies of the church." They

Evett Dumas (E.D.) Nix, United States marshal for Oklahoma Territory, Guthrie, 1893–96.

William "Old Man" Ransom, wealthy Ingalls resident, who owned a saloon and a livery stable.

"patronized the tables liberally [and] enjoyed themselves more than did the balance of the people in attendance." A few days later, two of the gang held up Hall's general store and escaped with $125. I.K. Berry and other leading merchants went to Guthrie "to see if another posse of marshals could be gotten into that country to clear the outlaws."

The Wild Bunch spread their operations west along the Cimarron. On January 3, 1894, Pierce and Red Buck Waightman held up the store and post office in the Dunker community of Clarkson above Cowboy Flat inside the Payne County line, looting the place of supplies, tobacco, cash, and all registered matter. Before the posse dust settled, four men led by Tulsa Jack held up a drug salesman named J.W. Pryer on Lost Creek south of Stillwater, taking his gold watch and sixty dollars. Next day, a Nix and Halsell Company employee was robbed west of Perkins by the same bandits. Obtaining only some pocket change, they scattered his samples in the roadway and warned him it would "mean his life" if they again caught him carrying so little money.

Meanwhile, Old Man Ransom filed a $10,000 suit in Payne County district court against Marshal Nix and his bondsmen for wounds received and damage to his buildings at Ingalls. Ransom alleged that, "as Nix's deputies precipitated the fight without giving the people warning," he was to blame, but the court held that Nix's men were "acting only in discharge of their duty." Neil Murray's claim to the U.S. Department of Justice for "crippling me for life" and "killing a good horse for me" also was denied.

Territorial newspapers labeled the gang's new outrages "another chapter" in its criminal history and declared, "The safety of citizens and property can never be achieved until its last member is dead or behind prison bars." The Stillwater *Eagle-Gazette*, as if oblivious of the responsibility of local authorities, asked, "Where, oh where, is Nix and his brave (?) deputies?" Others demanded that Nix "get a move on, or surrender the United States government to the bandits."

On January 16, Nix wrote Attorney General Olney, in part:

> The difficulties attending organization of men possess-
> ing the necessary qualifications to make a successful raid
> on the outlaws have been and now are the want of funds
> to equip and conduct such a campaign and also the want
> of adequate pecuniary inducement to tempt them. . .to
> expose themselves to almost sure death under the
> unerring aim of the bandits. . . .I earnestly recommend
> that the U.S. Marshal of Oklahoma be authorized to
> organize such a posse not to exceed fifteen men. . .that
> their expenses be limited to Three ($3.00) Dollars per
> diem of each man. . .and as extra expense the cost of
> preparation in the way of ammunition, hiring of horses,
> etc. [and that] the killing of horses owned or hired by
> the men be considered an expense they would be reim-
> bursed for. . . .
>
> While it is far preferable to adopt the proposition as
> stated, I will make the recommendation, if the Depart-
> ment deems it advisable to offer. . .in lieu of paying ex-
> penses. . .a reward of Five Hundred ($500) Dollars. . .for
> the capture [of each outlaw], dead or alive.
>
> I. . .desire to impress upon you the importance of
> early action, as people of the Territory are appealing to
> me daily for relief from. . .the depredations committed
> by this band of vicious and desperate characters.

At 3:30 P.M., January 23—as Nix awaited a response from Washington—Doolin, Newcomb, and Tulsa Jack entered the Farmers and Citizens Bank at Pawnee. The time lock on the vault was set for four o'clock, but Doolin did not wait as Grat Dalton had done at Coffeyville. He sacked up $262 left on the counter for the close of the day's business and forced cashier C.L. Berry outside to their horses. Doolin took the cashier up behind him to prevent citizens from opening fire on them. At the edge of town, he ordered Berry to "pile off," and the bandits escaped through the woodlands of Black Bear Creek into the Osage reservation.

Again, the Pawnee raid was the responsibility of local authorities, but the populace of that prosperous, fast-growing Outlet town complained all the way to the White

House. Maj. Frank Strong, general agent of the Department of Justice, sent Nix a biting inquiry. Nix, listing the known members of the Wild Bunch, fired back, "My deputies are ready at a moment's notice to take the field if Washington informs me that the Department has decided it would give a reward for each of the men I have mentioned, or in lieu thereof pay the expenses. . . . If impossible to have both. . . I would respectfully suggest it would be better to pay the expenses. . . . This gang is well organized. . . know every bridle path. . . are splendidly mounted and armed, and their protectors and friends are numerous. Any posse that may go after them will do so with the full knowledge that some of them will never return alive."

Major Strong did not reply, and Nix wired Attorney General Olney, "Will authority be granted me to pay expenses of posse as asked for in my letter of Janu. 16?" Olney requested by telegram "the amount of money required," and Nix promptly wired back, "Total cost will not exceed $1350, with strong probability that one-half that amount will suffice."

On February 26, Nix was authorized "expenses necessary." Any rewards would have to come from sources other than the government.

On March 10, a dispatch from Fort Leavenworth appeared in a newspaper of wide circulation in Oklahoma Territory, describing the intended movements of the army paymaster, the amount of money going to certain posts, and the means of transportation. An estimated $10,000 was being sent to Woodward by Wells Fargo to pay troops at Fort Supply. At one o'clock the morning of March 13, Doolin and Dalton (neither masked) rousted George W. Rourke, the Santa Fe station agent at Woodward, from his bed upstairs in the railroad hotel, marched him to the depot, forced him to open the railroad safe, and sacked up payroll packages containing $6,540. The pair then ran to the stockyards, where they were seen mounting two bay horses. A short distance from the yards they were joined by seven other riders, and all fled in a southwesterly direction.

Deputy Marshal Jack Love and a posse from Woodward,

Lt. Kirby Walker with a detail of twenty cavalrymen from Fort Supply, and veteran Indian scout Amos Chapman with a company of Cheyennes trailed the robbers into the badlands along the North Canadian. The robbers obtained fresh mounts at the Mose Zeigler ranch on Wolf Creek, crossed the Texas border, and vanished in the canyons and gulches near Lipscomb.

Marshal Nix and Chief Deputy Hale hurried to Woodward, conducted a three-day investigation and returned to Guthrie convinced that the entire Wild Bunch had participated. The gang now included Little Bill Raidler and Little Dick West.

Under date of March 20, Nix sent copies of the following directive to Heck Thomas, Bill Tilghman, and Chris Madsen:

> The Attorney General has authorized...$1500.00 from the appropriation for Extraordinary Expenses for the purpose of putting a stop to [these] gangs of Outlaws....
>
> I have selected you to do this work, placing explicit confidence in your abilities to cope with those desperadoes and bring them in—alive if possible—dead if necessary.
>
> Select your own men to assist you, and report to this office for further instructions as soon as possible.

At the ensuing meeting, Thomas was chosen to spearhead a search into the northeastern portion of the territory from his Guthrie headquarters, Tilghman the southeastern portion from his Bell Cow Creek ranch northwest of Chandler, and Madsen the western half from his home at El Reno. This triumvirate of famous manhunters would become known as Oklahoma's "Three Guardsmen."

Even as the lawmen mapped their campaign, a "new Dalton Gang" was being formed.

Following the Woodward robbery, Doolin and Bill Dalton had parted company, allegedly due to continued disagreement over the gang's leadership or a nine-way split of the $6,540 from the Woodward robbery (probably both). Bitter Creek Newcomb accompanied Dalton. Dalton's wife

Chris Madsen.

Bill Tilghman.

Heck Thomas.

and two children also disappeared from Kingfisher. Officers lost track of them near Ardmore.

About eight o'clock the evening of April 1, Dalton and Newcomb attempted to rob the store of W.H. Carr at Sacred Heart, a Catholic mission community above the Canadian near the Seminole border. Carr, a retired deputy marshal, resisted with pistol in hand, and was shot through the stomach. He managed to stay on his feet and wound Newcomb in the left shoulder as the pair ran into the darkness. Dalton escaped to his new hideout across the Canadian in the Chickasaw Nation. Bitter Creek fled into the Seminole country, where an Indian woman dressed his wound. Then he headed north to obtain medical attention at Ingalls.

Doolin had returned to the Ingalls area following his Woodward success to check on his pregnant wife, who was being cared for by Doctor Selph and Mary Pierce at the hotel. Dynamite Dick, Tulsa Jack, and Charley Pierce had been seen at the Dunn ranch. The Stillwater *Eagle-Gazette* of March 30 noted, "The people there live in constant terror of this gang . . . again making headquarters at certain places in town whose owners sympathize with them. . . . Several horses have been stolen in the vicinity."

Bitter Creek arrived too late to rejoin the Wild Bunch. The gang already had plotted its next raid and ridden north on the old Dalton Gang trails through the Cherokee Nation into the Ozarks. In mid-afternoon, May 10, Doolin, Pierce, Tulsa Jack, Dynamite Dick, Red Buck, Raidler, and Little Dick West robbed the bank at Southwest City, Missouri, of an estimated $4,000. In the exchange of gunfire with citizens as they swept out of town, a bullet broke the ankle of shoemaker Mart Hembree; Deputy Marshal Simpson F. Melton was hit in the thigh; Oscar Seaborn was shot through the hip; and his brother, J.C. Seaborn, former state auditor and one of Missouri's foremost citizens, was struck in the groin. The robbers escaped into the Grand River Hills of the Cherokee Nation and were soon hidden away in their Creek Nation cave on the Cimarron. J.C. Seaborn died a few days later, and the governor of Missouri posted a $1,700 reward for the capture of the gang or a "porportionate sum for any number of them," dead or alive.

The day Seaborn died—Monday, May 14—Arkansas Tom Jones, shackled and under heavy guard, was taken from the Guthrie jail to Stillwater for trial before Judge Frank Dale. Though Jones' case arose out of the killing of federal officers, he had been indicted for the deaths of Hueston, Speed, and Shadley on the territorial side of the court in November 1893, arraigned and returned to Guthrie early in February 1894. County Attorney King chose to prosecute the Hueston case, in which he had compiled the strongest evidence.

Shortly after court convened Tuesday morning, Judge Dale received a handful of letters purportedly written by Wild Bunch members warning him that he was in danger and that they intended to attack the courthouse and release their erstwhile accomplice. Sheriff Burdick provided guards for the judge to and from court, at the hotel where he was staying, and at the room in which he slept. King declined similar protection, instructing several specially appointed bailiffs to allow no one to enter the courtroom without being searched for weapons.

As the trial progressed, more threats came in, and Judge Dale considered the situation "sufficiently critical" to ask for federal reinforcements. A squad of marshals were sent to Stillwater at once, deputizing several citizens on the way. They stationed themselves on top of the courthouse with "long range guns" and at "key intervals" about the city, and vowed that any attempt to harm the court or rescue the prisoner would cost the perpetrators' lives.

Arkansas Tom basked in the light of not having been forgotten by his pals and "maintained that indifferent demeanor which has characterized his actions since his arrest." He did not take the witness stand. His attorneys contended it was "physically impossible" for him to have killed Hueston from the hotel attic "by punching holes through the shingle roof to take deadly and deliberate aim at the officer. . . occupied in defending himself"; that Jones had been "only an innocent bystander in the fight." Prosecutor King asked that the jury be allowed to "visit the

The reward for Bill Doolin's capture included $2,000 of U.S. Marshal E.D. Nix's own money.

scene and investigate for themselves." The request was granted. The jury made "a first hand survey of the location," and after deliberating all Saturday night, May 19, found a verdict of manslaughter in the first degree. On May 21, Judge Dale sentenced Arkansas Tom to fifty years in the penitentiary at Lansing. Jones' motion for a new trial and arrest of judgment was overruled. When he appealed to the territorial supreme court afterwards, the judgment of the district court was affirmed.

The Doolin gang raids following the Ingalls battle, Bill Dalton's antics on the Canadian, and the threats at Stillwater aroused the ire of Judge Dale. Upon returning to Guthrie at the end of the court term, he called Nix to his office and in effect countermanded the Thomas-Tilghman-Madsen directive: "Marshal...I have reached the conclusion that the only good outlaw is a dead one. It will simplify your problem...and probably save lives in the future [if] you will instruct your deputies to *bring them in dead.*"

It was the only order of its kind issued by an Oklahoma judge. Nix deposited $2,000 of his own money to supplement the expenses allowed by Washington. Rewards offered to date by banks, express companies, and the Missouri governor made Doolin alone worth $5,000.

THE WILD BUNCH FALLS 8

Ⅰ T WAS THE BEGINNING of the end for the Wild Bunch.

Bill Dalton was the first to fall. Ensconced with his family on the Houston Wallace farm near Elk, northwest of Ardmore, he organized his "new Dalton Gang" consisting of Wallace's brother Jim—an inept country loafer and wife-deserter late of Gregg County, Texas, using the alias George Bennett—and a pair of outlaw brothers, Big Asa and Jim Knight from Gregg County, near Longview. At three o'clock the afternoon of May 23, the quartet robbed the First National Bank at Longview of $2,000 in bills and a quantity of unsigned bank notes. Jim Wallace was killed by the city marshal. The label of an Ardmore store on the sweatband of the dead man's hat aided deputy marshals in tracing the remaining bandits to the Chickasaw Nation. On June 8, Dalton was slain by an Ardmore posse at his Elk hideout and a portion of the bank loot recovered. The Knights fled back to Texas and were intercepted by a sheriff's posse in Menard County. Big Asa was slain and Jim McKnight wounded, returned to Gregg County, and sentenced to life in prison. Dalton's wife and children accompanied his body to its last resting place in Merced County, California.

It had become increasingly difficult to obtain reliable information on the activity of the Wild Bunch since Arkansas Tom's conviction at Stillwater. Relying on rumors

Bill Dalton, in death.

among Doolin sympathizers along the Payne-Pawnee county line, Thomas, Tilghman, and Madsen, accompanied by Deputy Marshals Ed Morris, J.S. Prather, and William Banks of El Reno, chose what was believed an opportune time to move on the Dunn ranch.

They surrounded the two-story log house at daybreak. It was empty, but not the plank-covered storm cave nearby. They ordered the occupants to surrender. When there was no response, Thomas tossed a stick of dynamite that blew off the roof. Five men promptly appeared, hands in the air. None was the important quarry the marshals had expected. "It was not a dry haul however," Madsen remembered. "They were a second class lot of horsethieves. . . . They admitted four of Doolin's bunch had been there, but left the night before."

Morris, Prather, and Banks took the prisoners to Guthrie. Thomas, Tilghman, and Madsen continued a still hunt down the Cimarron.

Sheriff Frank Lake of Pawnee County tried a different tack. In the spring of 1894, he had prevailed upon his old friend Frank M. Canton (a former sheriff and stock detective in Wyoming during the Johnson County Rustlers War) to accept the position of undersheriff. Both men carried deputy marshal's commissions. The Dunn brothers had been disposing of stolen beef through a butcher, G.C. Bolton, who operated a meat market at Pawnee. Lake and Canton obtained enough evidence to have Bolton indicted and a warrant issued for Bee Dunn. Bee grew nervous and restless. He surrendered to the Pawnee officers, but proposed that, if the charges against him could be dismissed, he and his brothers would furnish information that would lead to the breakup of the Wild Bunch and Doolin's capture. After consulting with Marshal Nix, Lake and Canton agreed to the following terms: the Dunns must stop their thievery and harboring the outlaws, notify Lake and Canton at the moment any of the gang appeared in the section, and all reward money collected on any member of the Wild Bunch killed or captured would be paid to the Dunns after the actual expenses of the officers were deducted.

Months passed with periodic reports from the Dunns. The Creek Nation hideout near the confluence of Deer Creek and the Cimarron was discovered, but it soon became apparent that the cave had been abandoned as an assembling point and resting place for the outlaws. According to the Dunns, the gang had scattered—Dynamite Dick was in the Chickasaw Nation or Texas, Little Dick West in New Mexico. Doolin had not been seen since the raid on the Dunn ranch. He had put out feelers on giving himself up for some promise of clemency, but found Marshal Nix's terms unacceptable and had left the territory for climes unknown.

William Selph was the new postmaster at Ingalls. J.W. Ellsworth had moved his family to Lawson (later named Quay) on the Payne-Pawnee county line, where he operated a post office and store. Edith Doolin and her newborn son were living at Lawson with her parents. The Ellsworths were kept under surveillance and their mail watched by postal authorities.

There was one bright spot in the picture. Bitter Creek Newcomb had left "several hundred dollars" in Bee Dunn's care and sooner or later was "bound to drop in for his money."

Then, shortly before midnight, April 3, 1895, Newcomb, Pierce, Little Bill Raidler, Red Buck, and Tulsa Jack held up the southbound Rock Island train at Dover, eight miles north of Kingfisher, riddled the express car with lead, and wounded the messenger. The large, burglar-proof through safe containing $50,000 to pay U.S. troops in Texas could not be opened, so the bandits pilfered the mailbags and way safe. Finding no money, they went through the coaches, ordering the passengers to contribute in a couple of grain sacks, and rode into the night with some $400 cash and a quantity of jewelry valued at $1,000.

The train proceeded to Kingfisher, where the messenger received medical treatment and the engineer telegraphed Chris Madsen at El Reno. At 3:00 A.M., Madsen sped north on a special engine with twelve deputies and their horses in a boxcar coupled to the tender. Simultaneously, details of the robbery were dispatched to the Chicago, Rock Island and Pacific Railway headquarters at Topeka. The company

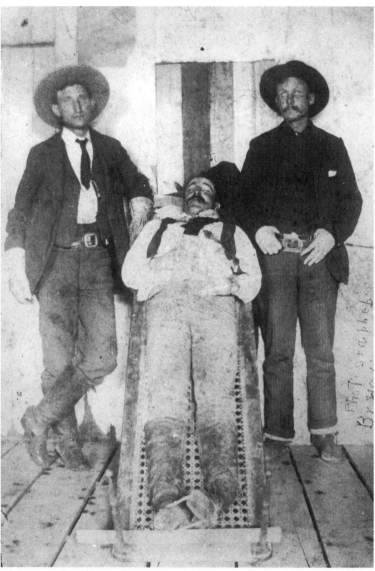

''Tulsa Jack'' Blake (on slab), flanked on left by Deputy Marshal William Banks and on right by Captain Prather.

offered $1,000 rewards for the arrest and conviction of each bandit and wired their descriptions throughout the territory.

Madsen's posse struck their trail at daybreak, followed it four miles west of Dover, north fifteen miles to the old boundary of the Cherokee Outlet, thence northwest into Major County. On Hoil Creek, near Ames, the robbers had stopped to breakfast at a farmhouse, then headed west into the sand hills toward the Cimarron. Madsen split his forces. With five men, he circled southwest to intercept the outlaws before they crossed the river. The second group, led by Deputies Prather and Banks, kept on the trail ahead.

At two o'clock in the afternoon, the Prather-Banks contingent topped a knoll on the edge of a small basin and saw the gang fifty feet below napping in a blackjack grove. A guard spotted the officers and gave the alarm. Without ceremony, the officers opened fire. The bandits ran to their horses and answered with a volley of lead. Banks killed Tulsa Jack with a Winchester ball that "entered his right side, passing through his heart and coming out under his left arm." Raidler was struck in one hand by a rifle ball, his horse wounded, and Red Buck's mount shot from under him before the outlaws, four of them on three horses, "escaped down a hollow which was not covered by the deputies."

Banks and Prather hired a farmer to haul Tulsa Jack's body to Hennessey, where he was photographed on an undertaker's board with the deputies standing on each side. It then was removed to El Reno and Oklahoma City, viewed by several hundred people before being identified, and finally returned to El Reno for burial.

The rest of the posse "pressed forward with Madsen from the scene of the fight." A few miles away, they came upon Raidler's horse, dead and spattered with blood from the outlaw's wounded hand. Later, they learned that one finger was bleeding so profusely that Raidler cut it off with a pocket knife and threw it away. At sundown, the posse reached the farm of an aged preacher named Godfrey, murdered by Red Buck, whom the minister "caught in his barnyard, taking his team." During the night, the gang crossed the Cimarron, obtained fresh horses from a stock farm near the settlement of Vilas, and fled into the Gyp Hills of Blaine County. There the robbers separated and tracking them became impossible. The posse returned to El Reno, "ragged and empty-handed."

The gang never reunited. Only Newcomb and Pierce remained together. Toward the end of April, they appeared at the Dunn ranch to pick up Bitter Creek's money.

Bee Dunn (so he claimed afterwards) "could not attempt" to warn Lake and Canton until the evening of May 1, when Newcomb and Pierce "went to Ingalls to get some girls and whiskey" to party at his log house. Bee left Dal Dunn at the ranch to "make excuses" should the outlaws return during his absence, and hurried to Pawnee. Lake and Canton, however, had gone to the George McElroy ranch southeast of Pawnee the previous afternoon to buy some grain for their horses and spend the night. That morning, they discovered their mounts had broken out of the corral and "had a long tramp" before finding them. Bee hunted for, but was unable to contact, the officers.

Meanwhile, John Dunn managed to inform Marshal Nix of the outlaws' presence. According to the Guthrie Leader, "Samuel Shaffer [an alias used by John Dunn] and two deputy marshals, well known all over the territory, but whose names THE LEADER is obliged to suppress [Tilghman and Thomas]...left this city with three possemen" the afternoon of May 1. By nightfall, they were "encamped near the Dunn place but in eye-shot of the house." The Leader continues:

> The bandits returned to the Dunn farm at 10 o'clock....An hour after they entered the house Bacchanalian orgies were in progress. The bold nocturnal riders were "out" or rather "in" for a time, with little thought of impending danger.
>
> The men [posse] surrounded the Dunn house...and at a given signal each man fired, alternately, one shot, as an alarm [warning to surrender]. Immediately a wild commotion ensued within the house...two lights

quickly flickered out. . . . A match was struck in the front room and simultaneously the door opened and Charley Pierce appeared with a Winchester in his hand. As his form loomed up a female voice was heard to cry: "Don't go, Charley!"

Pierce could not see his antagonists, but his figure with the lighted match in the room afforded a bullseye target for the officers, and in three seconds his breast was transformed into a lead mine. He fell directly back into the room; the leaden hail continued, bullets being planted in his arms, legs and even the soles of his feet.

Newcomb was endeavoring to climb out a window, unwisely shooting as he climbed. Three bullets were dexterously driven into his head, one tearing away a portion of his skull and brains. He fell back into the room with the stock of his Winchester shattered.

[The] Dunn boys were in the house. . . neither fired a shot, although one was wounded [slightly] by a random bullet. . . .

A young woman named Sallie Niles. . . had cried to Pierce when he stepped to his death. Nothing is known of her, but deputies surmise that she was Pierce's sweetheart. The woman was ordered out of the house and after making sure all was right, the officers entered, secured the bodies and loaded them into a wagon."

Shortly after two o'clock the afternoon of May 2, John and Dal Dunn arrived at Guthrie with the dead outlaws and claimed the rewards.

The buckshot in the soles of Pierce's feet led to the belief that he had been killed lying down. Despite the Dunns' story to the Guthrie newspapers, rumor spread that they had "got the bandits drunk" and killed them while they were "passed out or asleep." Tilghman and Thomas, in making their report to Marshal Nix, hardly clarified the matter. They knew nothing of the "Bacchanalian orgies"; they had been camped with their possemen on Council Creek, awaiting word from John Dunn that the outlaws had returned from Ingalls, when they heard "many shots fired." They rushed to the house and were met by the Dunn brothers "carrying shotguns and rifles" and saw Newcomb and Pierce "lying dead near the yard gate." Frank Can-

The Dunn cabin, scene of the demise of Newcomb and Pierce.

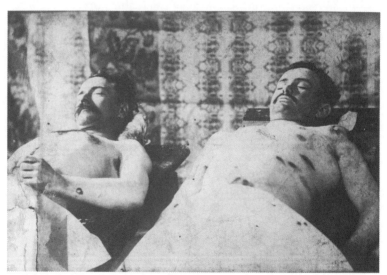

"Bitter Creek" Newcomb (left) and Charley Pierce (right) at undertakers in Guthrie after being slain at Dunn ranch house.

ton, arriving at Guthrie, fueled the controversy by declaring to the press that the Dunns had ambushed the bandits "after they rode into the yard and dismounted." He doubted Bee Dunn's efforts to contact him and Sheriff Lake and suspected that the Dunns knew how their horses had broken out of McElroy's corral.

Newcomb's body was claimed by his parents (then living in Cleveland County) and buried on their farm at Nine Mile Flats, west of Norman. Pierce was buried in the Boot Hill section of Guthrie's Summit View Cemetery at government expense. Their "cowardly assassination" by men they trusted aroused bitter feelings against the Dunns in the Ingalls community. Friends of the outlaws "openly swore revenge," and the Dunns "barricaded their place...made their ranch a veritable arsenal" for days before they felt "free of molestation."

Canton neither shared in the rewards nor received his manhunting expenses. He attempted to have the Dunns arrested for aiding and abetting the outlaws, but was thwarted by Nix. So he reactivated the cattle stealing charges against Bee Dunn and obtained additional warrants for his brothers. A rankled Bee rode into Pawnee. He waited in a stairway near Bolton's butcher shop until Canton came out of a restaurant where he had been serving some subpoenas. Stepping in front of the officer, he shouted, "Frank Canton, God damn you, I've got it in for you!" Bee's revolver was half drawn when Canton's bullet struck him in the forehead. He fell on the sidewalk, "dying and working the trigger finger of his right hand."

Bee was buried in the Ingalls cemetery despite protest by many citizens. A Pawnee grand jury declined to indict Canton since the killing was "plainly justifiable homicide."

Doctor Pickering notes in his diary:

> The feeling in Pawnee is all in favor of Canton. Past reputation is what hurts Dunn. All kinds of reports are afloat in regard to his past life at Ingalls. People are divided on the case. All was looking for Dunn to be killed but expected it to come from some of the remain-

ing outlaws. . . . I think it only a matter of time until more
of the Dunn boys are killed or they get Canton.

In fact, John, Dal, and George Dunn threatened to burn
Pawnee and ambush the deputy marshal. With many war-
rants for them outstanding, they finally left Oklahoma
Territory.

Toward the end of August, following the slaying of
Newcomb and Pierce, Tilghman learned through an Indian
informant that Little Bill Raidler was hiding at an old
Dalton Gang resting place on Mission Creek in the Osage
Nation, eighteen miles south of Elgin, Kansas. The outlaw
stayed in the timber in the daytime, ate and slept at night
at the Sam Moore ranch nearby. Moore, whose wife was
part Osage, farmed and ran cattle.

Tilghman, with Deputies W.C. Smith and Cyrus
Longbone of Bartlesville, reached the Moore ranch in late
afternoon, September 6. Raidler was not there, but Moore
"expected him anytime." He usually came up the lane past
the cattle corral at sundown. Smith and Longbone posted
themselves back of the house where the outlaw always
entered. Tilghman concealed himself in a log chicken roost
near the corral, armed with a double-barreled shotgun. At
dusk, Raidler came walking boldly up the path to supper.
As he passed the log structure, Tilghman stepped into view
and shouted, "Hands up!" The outlaw whipped out his
pistol and began running and shooting. Tilghman's
shotgun blast knocked him off his feet.

He was alive when the officers bent over him, but
bleeding badly from wounds in each side, his neck, head,
right arm, and wrist. Moore's wife brought a bucket of
water and some rags to staunch the blood. He was placed
on some hay in Moore's farm wagon and hauled to the
nearest doctor at Elgin. Two days later, he was taken by
train on a stretcher to Guthrie.

Raidler slowly recovered, was convicted of "attempting
to rob the United States mails" in the Dover train holdup,
and sentenced to ten years in the penitentiary at Columbus, Ohio. In prison, he suffered from locomotor ataxia
resulting from his wounds. He was paroled in 1903 because

of his illness, returned to Oklahoma, and died shortly afterwards.

By mid-December, Tilghman was hot on the trail of Bill Doolin.

Although it would not be known until many years later, Doolin had found sanctuary the summer of 1895 with Little Dick West on the horse ranch of the famed western novelist Eugene Manlove Rhodes in the San Andres Mountains of New Mexico. In late September, the bandit chief made his way to southern Kansas. He did not enter Oklahoma Territory, possibly because he heard of Raidler's capture and thought the Kansas border a safe place for his family to join him before returning to the San Andres.

In October, Edith Doolin loaded her personal effects and child into a covered wagon and headed north to Burden, a small community on the edge of the Flint Hills ranching district in east-central Cowley County. However, she became ill during her weary journey through the Osage and Doolin suffered a flare-up of the rheumatism which had developed in his left leg as a result of the bullet wound received in the Cimarron train robbery. They were forced to delay their westward trek. Both were attended by a local physician.

They pitched a tent near a fine spring about two miles west of town. Twice each week, Doolin went into Burden for supplies, disguised as a ragged, down-and-out Boomer using the name of Thomas Wilson. The family "affected such poverty" that, just before Christmas, a number of charitable ladies of Burden solicited a purse of money which they presented to the astonished "Mrs. Wilson."

Tilghman picked up Mrs. Doolin's trail in the Osage, where a "sick woman and her child" had camped briefly on the Kansas border. Finally, he learned that "relatives from Lawson" had been to Burden to "visit and care for her." Meanwhile, the unexpected attention of the citizens disturbed the crafty Doolin. He "packed up in the night" and vanished—"team, wagon and all, gone slick and clean."

Edith and the baby were still at the spring when Tilghman reached Burden. Night and day, he "kept vigil" on the camp and watched every train, but Doolin "did not show." On January 6, 1896, Edith and the baby boarded a train to Perry, going from there by hack to the home of her parents at Lawson.

Satisfied that Doolin would not return to Burden, Tilghman decided to trace him, and again got a clue that he "followed at once, with vigor"—Doolin and the physician who had treated him for his rheumatism had discussed the healing powers of the bath resorts in Arkansas. Tilghman searched eastward along the Kansas line. At a settlement in extreme southeastern Kansas, on January 12, he learned that a ragged stranger driving a famished looking team and a covered wagon had inquired the best route to Eureka Springs.

Tilghman reached Eureka Springs at 10:40 A.M., January 15. Here, in his words, is how the hunt ended:

> Walking up town, one of the first men I met was Doolin. He did not see me at the time and I soon learned that he was stopping at the Davy hotel under the name of Tom Wilson, the same name he had passed under at Burden.
>
> I then went to a carpenter and ordered a box made in which I could carry a loaded shotgun, deciding that I would disguise and, carrying the box under my arm, walk about until I met him, the box being arranged so that with a slight movement of the hand it would drop, leaving the gun in my hand ready for action.
>
> While the carpenter was making the box I determined to take a bath in the mineral waters from the spring and went to a bath house nearby. When I opened the door to step into the gentleman's waiting room...who should I see but Bill Doolin sitting on a lounge in the further corner...reading a paper. He looked up sharply...and seemed to me for a second that he recognized me but I walked briskly through the room and into the bath....
>
> Once inside the door I turned so I could watch him...his view was shut off by the stove...for several moments he watched the door through which I had passed...but finally relaxed...and returned to reading his paper. Now was my chance. With my gun in my hand I slipped quietly into the room up to the stove then

jumping around the stove...immediately in front of Doolin...told him to throw up his hands....He got up saying, "What do you mean, I have done nothing," but I grabbed his right wrist with my left hand as he raised it to get his gun and with my revolver leveled at his head ordered him to throw up his left hand. He put it up part way and then made a pass toward his gun but I told him I would shoot if he made another move....The room was full of men, but you should have seen them fall over each other to get out and in half a minute we were alone. I called to the proprietor to come and help me as I was an officer. He came tremblingly to the door and was finally persuaded to come over where we were. After two or three attempts he managed to get Doolin's vest open and take his revolver from under his arm and then he wanted to hand the revolver to me notwithstanding the fact that I had my own gun in my right hand. I told him to get out with it and he got, running into the street and holding the gun at arm's length....

I then said [to Doolin]: "Now, look at me; don't you know me?" He looked me in the eye and said: "Yes...you are Tilghman; where are your other men?" "Oh, they are all right," I said, and then told him he knew where he was wanted and it would be best for both of us to get out of that country at once. He agreed...said he didn't want to be known in that damned lynching country, and would go along....

I then put the nippers on him, got his gun and started for his hotel...got his effects...and left on the first train, not a soul there knowing who either of us were.

Tilghman wired Nix at Guthrie, "I have him. We be there tomorrow." Nix, Chief Deputy Hale, and Heck Thomas were waiting at the Santa Fe depot to escort captive and captor to the marshal's office through a scrambling, pushing, noon-hour crowd of thousands. After a brief interview with a large number of leading citizens and reporters, the prisoner was given dinner at the Hotel Royal, then lodged in the federal jail.

Tilghman was the man of the hour—lauded for making the quickest capture of one of the frontier's most notorious desperados by a single officer in western history.

Edith Doolin and her child made the long drive from Lawson to Guthrie in a one-horse open cart. She arrived in the territorial capital the afternoon of January 21. The meeting between man and wife was "very affecting."

During the pursuit of Doolin, Red Buck Waightman remained in the Cheyenne country, organizing a little "wild bunch" of his own. On September 1, 1895, he and a crony known only as "Charlie Smith" murdered Dewey County rancher Gus Holland and stole his cattle. On September 12, accompanied by two Texas fugitives, Joe Beckham and Elmer "Kid" Lewis, they held up the Santa Fe passenger train near Curtis, east of Woodward, failed to open the express safe, and escaped on the South Canadian. Smith dropped out of the picture. A month later, in October, Waightman, Beckham, and Lewis looted the Noyes general store at Arapaho, in Custer County, and again escaped. On December 4, they held up the Shultz and Aldrice store at Taloga and galloped away to Texas with a quantity of clothing and $100.

The trio took refuge on the Waggoner brothers' range on China and Beaver creeks in Wichita and Wilbarger counties, between Wichita Falls and Vernon. They fell in with Hill Loftus (a former Waggoner cowboy wanted for murder), and on Christmas day raided Waggoners' store near Vernon, beating a clerk half to death for refusing to tell where he kept the store's money. The gang then robbed Alf Bailey's store and post office a few miles south of Waggoners', and fled north across the Red River with $700 in merchandise, stamps, and money. A posse of Wilbarger County officers, Waggoner riders, and Texas Rangers, caught up with them in old Greer County. In the inevitable shootout, Beckham was killed; Loftus, Lewis, and a badly wounded Waightman escaped.

Loftus and Lewis returned to Texas, where Loftus was captured later. Lewis joined a former Oklahoma Territory outlaw named Foster Crawford. On February 25, 1896, the pair robbed a Wichita Falls bank and killed the cashier. Texas Rangers corraled them the next day without firing a shot and placed them in the Wichita Falls jail. On the night of February 27, three hundred irate citizens removed

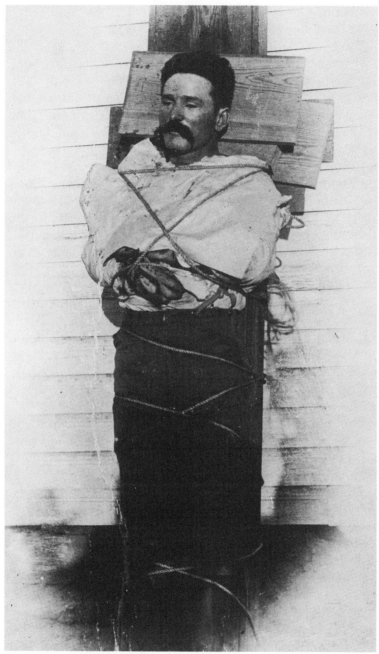

"Red Buck" Waightman, in death.

the bandits from their cells, took them to the front of the
bank, and hanged them from a telegraph pole.

Waightman managed to make his way back to the
Cheyenne country and recover from his wounds. On March
4, a posse of Custer County officers and citizens found him
hiding in a dugout on the claim of a friendly farmer five
miles west of Arapaho. When he refused to surrender, they
killed him. He was buried in the Arapaho cemetery at
county expense.

Upon receiving word of Red Buck's death, Doolin commented to a Guthrie reporter that it "showed how much
he himself had been maligned. . . the sins of others laid at
his door." Nonetheless, he agreed to plead guilty to the
killings at Ingalls on the promise of the U.S. district attorney to seek only fifty years, the same sentence given
Arkansas Tom.

On May 1, Tilghman and Deputy Marshal C.W. Reynolds
took Doolin to Stillwater for arraignment on the indictment.
He was "a great curiosity"; people from throughout Payne
County "thronged the courtroom to see the celebrated
outlaw." As Doolin gazed over the crowd, he recognized
a number of his Ingalls friends. He pleaded not guilty, was
bound over for trial without bond, and ordered returned
to the federal jail.

En route to Guthrie, Tilghman asked, "Bill, why did you
change your mind?"

Doolin replied, "Well, fifty years seemed a mighty long
time, and I believe I can beat the charges."

Tilghman did not realize what he meant.

A hint came a few weeks later. Dynamite Dick Clifton,
using the alias Dan Wiley, was arrested on a whiskey
charge at Rush Springs, Chickasaw Nation, by deputy marshals from the Eastern District of Texas and jailed at Paris.
He was wearing a celluloid collar and a heavy growth of
beard and protested the services of the barber. The shave
revealed a scar on his neck the size of a half-dollar, the
result of removing the rifle ball received in the Ingalls fight.
He was transferred to Guthrie on a federal murder warrant,
June 22. Doolin saw him when he was booked in, and the
expression on the bandit chief's face was "one of both terror

and excitement.'' As Dynamite was being locked in a separate cell, he admonished, ''For God's sake, Dick, stand pat!''

Apparently, no one took notice.

A jailer and two guards attended the prison in the daytime, and two guards from 6:00 P.M. until morning. The jail entrance was reached by an outside stairs ten feet above the ground level of the building. The office, or receiving corridor, twelve feet deep and running the width of the building, was divided from the prison area by iron bars that extended from floor to ceiling. A big, barred door opened into the bull pen where the prisoners were allowed freedom in the daytime. Through the door on the left were two blocks of cells where the most dangerous inmates were kept. Across the back of the bull pen and part way along the walls on each side ran a tier of steel cages where the other prisoners were locked up between eight and nine o'clock at night. Doolin and Dynamite Dick were kept in the front block of cells.

At 8:45 P.M., Sunday, July 5, night guard Joe Miller deposited his revolver in a box beside the corridor door, and night guard J.T. Tull let him into the bull pen to lock up the prisoners. A bucket of water sat at the right of the door on the corridor side, where the prisoners could reach through the bars to get a drink. They usually filled tin cans to take to their cages, so Miller paid little attention to George Lane (a hulking Cherokee-Negro awaiting trial for selling whiskey in the Osage), who stood in the corner, reaching through to the bucket. Walter McLain and Lee Killian (serving sentences for whiskey peddling in the Pawnee country) and W.H. Jones (charged with counterfeiting) were waiting with cans nearby. Lane mumbled about not being able to reach the water, and Miller turned to check the position of the pail.

Quick as a flash, Lane seized Miller and pinned his arms to his side. McLain, Killian, and Jones rushed Tull through the doorway and tore his revolver from his shoulder holster. Doolin leaped after them and grabbed Miller's revolver from the box. He forced Tull to open the combination locks on the front cell block, releasing Dynamite Dick

and eight others. Thirty-five prisoners still in the bull pen
were invited to join them. When they refused, Tull was
locked in a cell, Miller in the bull pen, and the thirteen
escapees ran downstairs. By the time the alarm was spread,
all had vanished helter-skelter into the darkness.

Doolin and Dynamite Dick fled north along the Santa Fe
tracks. They met a young man and a girl returning to
Guthrie in a buggy drawn by a fine bay mare, left the couple
on foot, abandoned the buggy on a country road farther
north, and galloped away on the mare.

Most of the other escapees eventually surrendered or
were captured. For weeks, posses combed Cowboy Flat,
the Cimarron, the Flat Iron country, and the Ingalls area
with no trace of Doolin. He and Dynamite Dick had
separated. Dynamite reportedly was seen in the old Sac
and Fox reservation with Little Dick West, who had
recently returned from New Mexico. Citing Doolin's "poor
state of health," many believed he had left the territory.

Heck Thomas, however, did not believe Doolin would
leave without his wife and child. He engaged the services
of Tom and Charlie Noble, two young blacksmiths at
Lawson whose shop sat within "rock tossin' distance" of
the Ellsworth store. Promised a share of the rewards, the
Noble boys agreed to keep an eye on the outlaw's wife.
Thomas continued a still hunt along the Cimarron, accompanied by his son Albert (who often rode in his posses)
and a Cherokee Indian deputy, Rufus Cannon.

On Sunday night, August 23, Doolin visited his wife.
Early the next morning, riding the mare taken during the
Guthrie escape, he "passed down the road west" into the
timber on Eagle Creek. Later, the Nobles watched Edith
Doolin and her father load a wagon with a plow, some
household goods, and her personal effects.

Thomas got the word at his camp below the Cimarron,
where he had been checking a lead on Dynamite Dick and
West. With Albert and Deputy Cannon, he made a "hard
ride" twenty-five miles almost due north, met the Noble
boys near Lawson at sundown, and kept the Ellsworth
place "under surveillance through field glasses" until
twilight. Doolin and his wife were at the stable back of the

N

A. Door to bullpen
B. Steel cells
C. Combination boxes to cells B
D. Box where Miller put his revolver
E. Booking desk
F. Bullpen
G. Small cells
H. Corridor
I. Stairway to basement
J. Water bucket
K. Large front doors

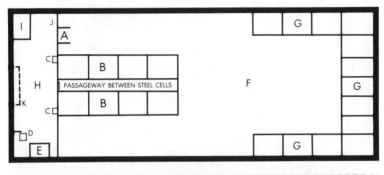

U.S. Jail, Guthrie, O.T., from which Bill Doolin made his famous escape, July 1896.

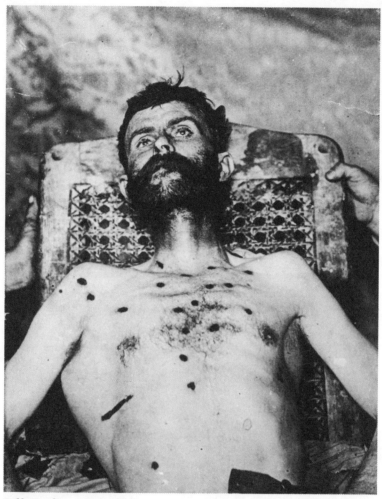

Bill Doolin, in death.

store, "in conversation...waiting for darkness to make
their departure."

At nightfall, the posse crawled into a cane patch at the
side of the road to Eagle Creek. They "waited a long time
without seeing anyone," but there was "considerable stir"
about the store and residence. Shortly before midnight,
Doolin came out of the stable. He placed his wife and child
in the wagon. Edith took the reins, with instructions to
meet him on the other side of the creek.

Here is Heck Thomas' version of what happened next:

> Doolin's wife had told him some of the neighborhood
> boys had been spying around and that someone was
> around there that night. Doolin said he would just scare
> hell out of them...shoot them up a little if he saw
> them....He could have made his escape on the open
> roads, north, south, east...or through the pasture to the
> high hills northwest....
>
> Well, he came right down the lane, walking slow in
> the bright moonlight, Winchester in both hands, well
> out in front of him...in position to shoot. He was sure
> on the prowl....I hollered at him...he shot at me and
> the bullet [missed]. I had let one of the boys have my
> Winchester and had an old No. 8 shotgun. It was too long
> in the breech and I couldn't handle it quick so he got
> another shot with his Winchester...jerked his pistol and
> some of the boys thought he shot once with it. About
> that time I got the shotgun to work and the fight was
> over.

As Doolin fell, his wife cried out, "Oh, my God, they
have killed him!" She "carried on to a great extent," but
neither she nor any of her family ventured to the scene.

A local farmer furnished the mules and wagon that
hauled the buckshot riddled corpse to Guthrie, where it
was viewed by an "immense throng." Edith Doolin com-
posed a poem about her husband, which was printed post
card size on the back of his photograph and sold at twenty-
five cents each, the proceeds to be used for burial expenses.
The government, however, bore that cost. Doolin was
buried in Summit View Cemetery alongside Charley Pierce.

''Dynamite Dick'' Clifton, in death.

His wife and her hack driver were the only mourners, and "outside of two attaches of the Marshal's office and cemetery attendants," there were "few lookers-on."

Less than two months after the Wild Bunch leader's death, Dynamite Dick and Little Dick West raided a store at Carney, in Lincoln County, and the Sac and Fox agency near the Creek Nation border. By June of 1897, they were riding with a comic-opera quartet out of the Pottawatomie country consisting of lawyer-gone-wrong Alphonso J. "Al" Jennings, his brother Frank, and two Tecumseh plow-pushers, Morris and Pat O'Malley. Following an unproductive holdup of a Santa Fe train at Edmond in August, an aborted attempt on the Katy railroad south of Muskogee, a bungled attack on a Rock Island express and mail car north of Chickasha, and an October looting of the Crozier and Nutter general store at Cushing of winter clothing valued at $150, the gang took refuge at the Spike S ranch on Snake Creek, near Sapulpa.

Disgusted with the gang's accomplishments, Dynamite Dick and West left the Jenningses and O'Malleys after the Cushing performance. West headed for the Deep Fork of the Canadian to visit a Creek girl friend. Dynamite Dick rode off to an old hiding place west of Checotah.

Deputy Marshals George Lawson and Hess Bussy of the Eufaula District learned of his coming. On November 7, after "laying out in the hills several days familiarizing themselves with his beat," the officers "pulled down on their man on the trail and ordered him to surrender." But the outlaw "obeyed not...raised his rifle and fired." A ball from Lawson's rifle broke his arm and knocked him off his horse. He dropped his Winchester and fled into the timber. The officers followed his bloody trail to an Indian cabin. Again Dynamite refused to surrender. When the officers threatened to burn the cabin, he leaped from the doorway, his six-shooter blazing. He died in a hail of lead and was buried at Muskogee at government expense.

On the night of November 29, a posse of federal deputies headed by veteran Indian Territory marshal James Franklin "Bud" Ledbetter flushed the Jennings gang at the Spike S ranch. Morris O'Malley was captured; Pat O'Malley (right leg slashed by a rifle ball), Al Jennings (a bullet in his left thigh), and Frank Jennings (clothing riddled by buckshot but with no serious injury) escaped in the Snake Creek bottoms. They commandeered a team and wagon from two Indian boys in the hills, drove through Okmulgee to Checotah, obtained medical attention, and outfitted the wagon with blankets and provisions for a trek into Arkansas. Shortly before daybreak, December 6, Ledbetter and his posse met the fugitives at a crossing on nearby Carr Creek and took them without firing a shot. All were indicted and tried in the Southern District of Indian Territory for the express and mail robbery on the Rock Island. Al Jennings was sentenced to life imprisonment at Columbus, Ohio; Frank and the O'Malleys received five years each in the penitentiary at Leavenworth.

The capture of the Jennings gang and killing of Dynamite Dick caused Little Dick to bid his girl friend good-bye and seek safety among settler acquaintances in Oklahoma Territory. Around Christmas time, using the alias Dick Smith, he hired out as a farm hand on the Ed Fitzgerald place on Cottonwood Creek, five miles southwest of Guthrie. Virtually in the shadow of the U.S. marshal's office, West thought it the most unlikely spot that officers would look for him. In the spring of 1898, he found extra work on the adjoining farm of Harmon Arnett. Then he made the mistake of asking Arnett to join him in a robbery.

On April 6, Mrs. Arnett went to Guthrie and passed the information and West's description to the wife of the district clerk, who told Logan County sheriff, Frank Rinehart. Rinehart told Deputy Marshals William D. Fossett, Tilghman, and Heck Thomas. The officers reached the Fitzgerald place at three o'clock the morning of April 8.

Little Dick was not there, but his horse was in the corral. The officers separated, Fossett and Rinehart going to search the Arnett farm. Tilghman and Thomas remained at Fitzgerald's. About daylight, they sighted West scouting along the timber toward Arnett's house, and started in pursuit. Fossett and Rinehart, approaching the house from the front, saw the outlaw enter the breezeway. West spotted them at the same moment, disappeared behind a shed at

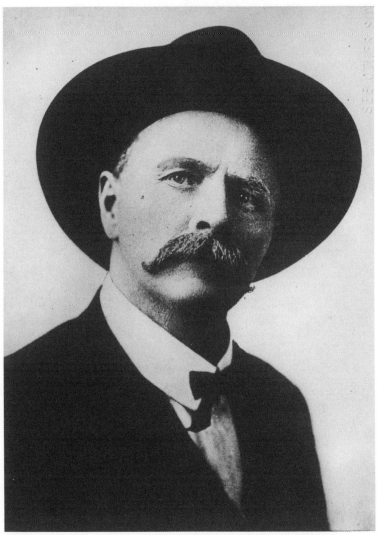

U.S. Deputy Marshal James Franklin "Bud" Ledbetter.

"Little Dick" West, in death.

the rear, and began walking toward the barn. Fossett yelled that he wanted to speak with him. West turned, drew his six-shooter and fired three shots close to the officers' heads. The outlaw then ran for the barn lot fence. A bullet from Fossett's Winchester and two blasts from Rinehart's double-barreled shotgun brought him down. He died, lying on his back, his cocked six-shooter in his hand.

It had taken nearly four years to carry out Judge Frank Dale's edict.

INGALLS PASSES
INTO HISTORY 9

INGALLS TRIED TO PUT itself back on the road to
respectability.

On April 28, 1894, the "upright citizens of the town and
vicinity" met at the schoolhouse, and after "short speeches
by the chair and others," adopted the committee report as
follows:

> Whereas: The town of Ingalls has a hard name for
> outlaws and thieves, all because of the fight last
> September. . .a few individuals violating and disturb-
> ing the peace. . .and other things not in conformity with
> law and order. Therefore, be it
>
> Resolved, That we, the citizens of Ingalls and com-
> munity, condemn and discountenance any of these
> things and are heartily ashamed that it has been done.
>
> 2nd. That we will do all in our power that is lawful
> to put a stop to all unlawful deeds by striving to bring
> all violators of the law to justice.
>
> 3rd. That the county papers be requested to publish
> these resolutions.

The *Eagle-Gazette* of May 17 printed the report, and an
account of another meeting held on May 7 appeared in the
Oklahoma State Sentinel (successor to the Stillwater *Hawk*)
on May 10: "A total of 45 citizens attended. . . .Due notice

134

and warning was given to the toughs who have been stealing, shooting, and raising disturbances. . . . They try to do
a great deal of this on the credit of those who were called
the outlaws [but] there has not been one of the gang in Ingalls for two months.

"The citizens of this vicinity have stood all of that kind
of work they are going to."

Though the real outlaws had gone, many who admired
them tried to emulate them and disregarded the committee's demands.

A drummer and his young son visiting the town in June
found that they could not finish their business until next
day. Uneasy about staying at the hotel, they set up a tent
and prepared to bed down for the night. "We had driven
a long way and were tired," the son recalled, "so we turned
in early. Shortly after dark guns started firing all over the
place. We could hear bullets whizzing through the air and
striking objects around us. Some went through our tent,
but fortunately neither of us was hit."

The outside press did not help matters. Territorial cor-
respondents labeled Ingalls the "badlands" of the new
country and concocted lurid stories. Within a month after
the killing of Bill Dalton near Ardmore, a dispatch
originating with the Norman *Democrat* alleged that "six
men rode into Ingalls on the night of July 3, and, declaring that Dalton had been betrayed by Saloonkeeper
Nicholas, proceeded to demolish his place. The saloon
was a wreck within three minutes. It is said that Nicholas
gave certain officers the information as to Dalton's
whereabouts."

Of course, there was no man by the name of Nicholas
operating a saloon in Ingalls. The *Sentinel* editor further
discredited the yarn by reprinting it alongside a list of the
town's businessmen at that time: Robert Beal, William Call,
Bradley & Dean, and W.B. Selph, grocers; Ketchum,
shoemaker; Pierce, liveryman; Dr. Briggs, druggist; Sherman Sanders, barber; Murray and Strange, saloons; Dent
Ramsey, hardware; Mrs. Thomas, restaurant; A. Catliff, dry
goods; William Wagner, blacksmith; Pierce, hotel; Selph,
Briggs, and Pickering, doctors; and Ingalls Milling Com-

pany, W.E. Groton, president.

Doctor Call had ceased practice and entered the grocery business east of the hotel. Bradley & Dean, formerly of Tyro, Kansas, had opened a grocery store and lunch counter adjoining the Thomas restaurant; Strange had acquired Vaughn's saloon; Catliff, of Texas and Arkansas, had been in Oklahoma only a short time and purchased Perry's drygoods; the Ingalls flour mill, "fitted up with the latest improved machinery and more qualified than any other mill in the territory," commenced serving the public on August 15.

Stories of Ingalls' violence did not have to be invented. On September 30, 1894, Andy Brazwell wounded Neil Murray in the head with a revolver bullet. Doctor Pickering describes the cause and outcome:

> They had been having a lot of trouble over a gambling debt.... There was a show in town and there was lots of drinking. The show did not open [that] night for fear of trouble [and] there came up a storm in the evening. Murry & Andy went to Bradley & Deans grocery to get a lunch all aperant in good humor. Just as they were setting it out Andy pulled his gun & shot then skiped out. He was gone probely 2 or 3 mo & they complemised [compromised] and he came back. He then started in the saloon business.

The rough element continued uncontrolled. The *Sentinel*'s correspondent at Ingalls provided this account of the well-publicized "Johnson and Culbertson Fight" of Thursday, February 14, 1895: "It commenced in Bradley & Dean's store and lasted about a quarter of an hour. We are liberal here when we have entertainment. We have it free for all. It wound up in the street, by one man being hog tied, the constable scratched and bruised up, and some others with their eyes gouged, ribs broken, and hair pulled out, but nothing serious happened."

The intensity of the fight is indicated in this paid advertisement sent shortly afterwards: "NOTICE: The following described property found...on the street after the free for all: Six sacks of smoking tobacco, one dozen cob pipes,

Baseball team at Ingalls in the 1890s. (Town buildings in background.)

some damaged; four walking sticks, three and one half sets of artificial teeth; three dozen hair pins, two pairs of spurs, one quart of alcohol, three hymn books, four pairs of eye glasses, all broken; three rawhide whips, two boxes of cartridges, and about two quarts of suspender buttons.''

The Johnson-Culbertson affair was capped by ''another day of revelry,'' February 16: ''If a stranger had happened into Ingalls Saturday he would have thought he was in Dodge City or some other frontier town in the early days. The drunkenness, hollowing, screaming, cursing, running horses, and blackguarding was a disgrace and scandal to the community.

''The citizens are circulating a petition to make up money to hire an attorney to prosecute some cases. They say if their county attorney won't do it, they will hire someone who will.''

Even the devil appeared to be taking a toll. On April 8, Ingalls suffered its first fiery disaster. Doctor Pickering writes:

> About 7:30 P.M. the alarm was given that Pierces Livery Barn was on fire. I ran down found the barn as good as gone most of Murrys things carried out of his house [next door]. They had given up hope of saving it. I and Jim Vaughn went on top of it & by hard work saved it and by doing this saved the whole row [of buildings]. There were 5 head of horses burned in the barn 2 of Pierces 2 of the Pawnee Mail mans and 1 driven here by Lawyer Hale of Stillwater. The origin of the fire was probely incendiary. No clews to who did it. No insurance on anything.

Gunplay was standard fare during the closing months of 1895.

On September 25, Henry Foot and Frank Carpenter were charged with the murder of Levi P. Slaybaugh. The Stillwater *Populist* of October 10 said, ''Foot was by the probate court of Payne county in June of this year adjudged insane and a guardian appointed for him. Carpenter is charged with abetting and inciting Foot to commit the of-

fense. . . . Foot by his guardian entered a plea of not guilty
[when] arraigned before Justice of the Peace Johnson
Whiles. . . hearing continued to the 4th of October.''
  Doctor Pickering details the case:

> Levi Slaybaugh [was] one of the best men in the county.
> Charley Slaybaugh ran in the strip [Outlet] and located
> a claim. Carpenter wanted it and got Foot (who was his
> uncle and half witted) to contest Charley. He got beat
> at Perry [land office]. He then appealed. In the mean-
> time Carpenter went off on a visit (he had built a $500
> house on the claim). While he was gone Foot settled with
> Slaybaugh for $50 and gave a clear release then he left.
> When Carpenter came back he hunted up Foot and took
> him to county seat & had him judged insane & was ap-
> pointed Guardian for him and was trying to get the con-
> test reopened. [Levi] Slaybaugh on the eve of 25th was
> on creek with Charley cutting poles to fix corn crib. Foot
> & Carpenter went to them & picked a quarrel. Foot shot
> the old man. Charley then knocked him [Foot] down
> with an ax & Carpenter ran off. If it had not been for the
> Slaybaugh boys pleedings Carpenter would have been
> linched that night. He had a preliminary before Judge
> Whiles a poor demented fool (if I must call him such)
> who turned him loose & bound over a crazy man.

  The *Gazette* of Thursday, October 31, reported ''another
shooting scrape at Ingalls last Monday morning when Dr.
Briggs received a severe wound from a gun in the hands
of his son. . . . Young Briggs immediately fled and has not
been seen since.''
  Doctor Pickering writes:

>   Dr. Briggs and his son Rob a boy probely 20 yr old
> got into a quarrel at the breakfast table & Rob shot
> two times in the house. The old man got out onto the
> street & was running for dear life. Rob shot at him again
> hitting him in the left arm. He would of shot more but
> his mother and Mrs Murry got hold of him & he gave
> up. I cut the ball out of his fathers arm a few minutes
> later. It was a 45. The boy left & I suppose this is the
> last of [it].

Ingalls partially solved its dilemma by adopting an ordinance prohibiting "the selling of malt, vinous and spiritous liquors within the corporate limits" and closing its saloons. The *Gazette* observed, "Why the citizens do not want saloons is plain to be seen. The parents wish to raise their boys as best they can and by barring the liquor selling right they can do so with less trouble to themselves."

Later, the *Gazette* questioned, "How does it come that dozens of Stillwater men and boys who go to Ingalls sober return home with a tremenduous jag? Is it possible that Ingalls is running her saloons on the Kansas plan and doing business under the name 'Drug Co.' 'Ingalls Pharmacy,' with an ounce of quinine and a bottle of Groves chill tonic on her shelves while behind the prescription case is a little book which by signing and depositing a dollar in the coffers one can get a pint or a half pint of that which makes men and boys walk the street light headed."

Nevertheless, reports from the town the next couple of years were of business development and social change.

"The Ingalls grist mills ground 1700 bushels of corn since March."

"The Texas hogs that have been brought in here are doing well and taking on fat in a manner that rejoices the owners."

"Anyone desiring to pick cotton can find employment out this way as nearly every farmer is calling for help."

"Several stores are being enlarged and have changed hands."

Dent Ramsey, for example, divorced his wife shortly after the Ingalls battle; he then married Preacher Perry's daughter, Ora, sold out to a man named Parmley, and moved to Pawnee, where he became mayor and reentered the hardware business in partnership with his new father-in-law. Bullet-punctured structures "attracting too many visitors" were torn down or moved to the town's new

Ingalls' new business section, early 1900s.

Smith & Pickering store in Ingalls, early 1900s. Note grain mill and storage facilities in background (far left).

business section along First Street. More importantly, "Our
religious interest is getting on in good shape."

Doctor Pickering concludes his diary:

> The first church building was commenced [at the
> southwest edge of town] the last of Feb 98. Johnathan
> West had contract to build it for $385.00 It has changed
> the plans some which adds more to the cost of the
> building. It is being built by Methodist people ME North.
> Mr West has just finished a fine two story school
> building for the Ingalls district at a cost of over $1200.00
> two rooms below & hall above. There will be several
> good buildings put up this spring.

Most of the labor and a large share of the money and
materials for the Methodist structure was donated. Henry
Pierce and Harrison Clark "Harry" Whipple (another Ingalls pioneer residing near the site) hauled the lumber
from Guthrie.

The Baptists built a church across the street, and a Christian church was constructed on the H.H. Hammock farm
to the southwest. All three churches reportedly were "com-
fortably filled" each Sunday.

The Christian church was the most elaborate, completed
"at no small expense. . .the donations liberally made by
numerous helpers over the county. . . .and very handsome-
ly furnished." But relations between the "progressive" and
"non-progressive" branches of the denomination were not
rosy. According to the *Gazette* of April 18, 1901, the non-
progressives "adhered to the old land marks of Alexander
Campbell"; the progressives "took up new manners and
in a way thought by the non's to be revising the church
discipline and were very critically censured by them."
Trouble grew until the matter of purchasing leaflets came
up in a business meeting and the progressives and non-
progressives disagreed on the kind of materials the
organization should use in their Sunday school work. On
the night of April 11, the building was "blown into
atoms. . . .A dynamite fuse was found in the debris, leaving no doubt as to how it was so completely demolished."

Though no person or group was ever identified with the

The Christian Church southwest of Ingalls was blown up by dynamite in April 1901.

act, the *Gazette* assumed it was "the work of one of these quarreling branches" and decried that "such envious feeling should creep out of a small trouble causing valuable property to be destroyed and the community in which it took place disgraced in church circles."

In 1901, the O.K. Hotel—the last grim reminder of the Ingalls battle—was dismantled in sections and moved to Stillwater, where it was reassembled as the Globe Hotel in the 500 block on South Main. Later, it served as an apartment house, then a family residence. Finally, in a state of decay, the building was partly cut off at the rear, moved to 812 South Hester street and remodeled into a story and a half duplex. Today the structure retains little of its original appearance—white shingled, with dormers, a railed porch roof, and modern siding. One memento remains—a small hole in one door patched with metal, allegedly made by a bullet intended for Arkansas Tom.

The Pierce family also moved to Stillwater in 1901, where Henry dealt in livestock and managed the Globe. On the night of February 19, 1905, after delivering eighteen head of mules to a buyer at Perry, he was shot to death and robbed a block east of the Santa Fe tracks near the old Kinnick feed barn.

It was the railroad that finally killed Ingalls.

In 1899, the Eastern Oklahoma Railway Company (a subsidiary of the Atchison, Topeka and Santa Fe) completed a line from Guthrie to Cushing, providing rail service to Coyle, Goodnight, Vinco, and Ripley just south of Ingalls, below the Cimarron. Ingalls wanted a line built directly north from Ripley into Pawnee County. After much persuasion, fund raising, and some clever trading by Stillwater, Eastern decided to bend a 40.4-mile branch through the county seat to Esau Junction east of Pawnee. Work was commenced on a railroad bridge across the Cimarron in late February 1900. By the end of March, the track layers had passed through Mehan, bridged Boomer Creek at Stillwater, and were headed north to Glencoe Station. Yost (Youst) Lake was constructed by the Santa Fe as an intermediate watering hole for its iron horses that, by 1902, were plying the Ripley-Pawnee route daily.

Education of the young in the Ingalls community was not neglected. Students and teachers in front of school buildings at Ingalls, early 1900s.

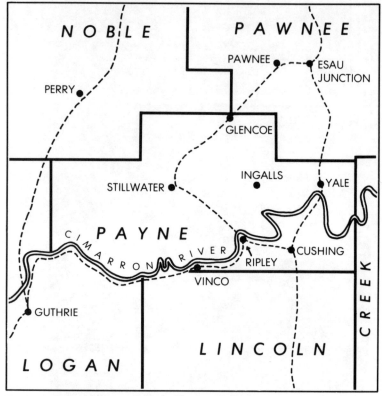

Route of the Eastern Oklahoma Railway bypassing Ingalls.

Ingalls still expected a railroad after surveyors of the Kansas Midland or Missouri Pacific were seen making studies in the Lawson area. That hope, too, was dashed. Building from a point near Agra, in Lincoln County, to Esau Junction on its way to the Osage in 1903 and 1904, the Katy gave Cushing its second railroad and added Yale to the list of towns with rail service in Payne County. Ingalls residents not already drawn away to Ripley and Stillwater moved in groups to Yale and Cushing.

However, many of the people who had known Arkansas Tom Jones at the time of the Ingalls battle were still around in the spring of 1904, when the Rev. Sam Daugherty, pastor of a Methodist church at Greenville, Texas—Tom's brother—came seeking endorsements for the outlaw's pardon.

A couple of months previous, Arkansas Tom had come to the assistance of a Lansing, Kansas, prison guard and prevented the escape of Bill Rudolph, a Missouri killer, then under sentence of death and awaiting execution. Tom had received a fair education before taking up cowboy life in Texas, and it aided him in becoming one of the prison's principal bookkeepers. His action in preventing Rudolph's escape won him high praise by prison and state authorities. Warden Edward Jewett and several other officials had acquiesced to a pardon application directed to Oklahoma's territorial governor, Thompson B. Ferguson.

Among those contacted by the Reverend Daugherty was Billy McGinty, who had married Mollie Pickering and was living at Ripley. Billy recalled, "I told the minister, 'I once warned Tom about getting in with the Doolin crowd. He made it plain that it was none of my business then, and it's none of my business now. You ask Tom if he wasn't warned next time you see him.'

"I wouldn't sign the application, but a few Ingalls men did."

The move met with vigorous protest. Strong individual remonstrances were drawn up by officials involved in Arkansas Tom's capture and trial and by relatives and friends of those who fell in battle with the Wild Bunch.

The *Stillwater Advance* of June 9 expressed the opinion

of Payne County citizens in general:

> Dick Speed, young Simmons, Tom Hueston and Lafe
> Shadley sleep the long slumber of death in untimely
> graves, as courageous heroes as ever fell before the shots
> of desperadoes. . . . To talk about a pardon to this man
> Jones is to insult every believer in law and order in
> Oklahoma. . . .
>
> It is true that the comrades saved by his marksman-
> ship that September morning are no longer in this
> world. . . one by one they have vanished into the earth
> and polluted her fair bosom with their black
> presence. . . but everyone knows the cowardly methods
> of assassination employed by Jones in the slaughter of
> [those who] gave their lives for the enforcement of
> law. . . . The sentence of fifty years was merciful; if he
> had been given less the probabilities are that his carcass
> would have adorned a pole in the vicinity of the county
> jail the next morning.
>
> We have too much faith in Governor Ferguson to
> believe that he would lend a willing ear. . . in this case.
> Pardons were intended for those who were convicted im-
> providently or in whose cases there exists extenuating
> circumstances. This man is four times guilty of murder,
> and it is not a case where pardon would be justified.

Governor Ferguson took a jaundiced view of the matter.
His successor, Frank Frantz of Rough Rider fame, review-
ing the case in 1906, also declined to free the unpopular
outlaw.

On November 16, 1907, Oklahoma and Indian territories
became a single state. Charles N. Haskell was inaugurated
as the first state governor. Early in his administration, the
legislature provided for a state prison, and 520 territorial
convicts were transferred from Lansing to the old federal
stockade at McAlester. Among them was Arkansas Tom.

In the interim, the Rev. Sam Daugherty had secured
signatures throughout Kansas, Oklahoma, and Texas.
However, at a hearing in Guthrie on April 16, 1908, executive clemency again was denied in the face of ''stiff op-
position from Payne County citizens unwilling to forget
the wanton killing of three deputy marshals'' and hostile

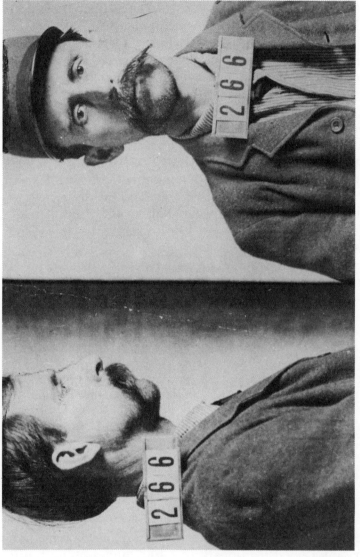

"Arkansas Tom" Jones, No. 266, Kansas State Penitentiary Lansing, Kansas.

to a pardon policy which "looks to the feeling and interest only of the criminal."

Finally the indefatigable Daugherty visited E.D. Nix, then living in St. Louis and dealing in investments, stocks and bonds. Time had mellowed the ex-marshal's feelings, and he was impressed with Tom's "fine record" during fourteen years of incarceration. He recommended Tom's release and influenced other federal officers who had participated in his prosecution to do the same. In 1910, during the last months of Governor Haskell's regime, paroles and pardons were granted to a number of life termers and others serving sentences for homicides of various degrees. One pardon, "smothered and not discovered" until Haskell left office, bore the name "Roy Daugherty, alias Tom Jones."

Shortly after leaving prison, Arkansas Tom came to Ripley to see Billy McGinty, who recalled:

> He didn't blame me for not signing his papers—just wished he had taken my advice. My wife was in the hospital with a fever and the three boys and me were having a rough time cooking and all. Well, Tom took over. He was a good cook and kept the boys in school several weeks before Mollie was well enough to come home.
>
> The oil boom had hit Yale, Cushing and Drumright, in Creek County. Tom went to Drumright and ran a short order restaurant for a while, then started keeping books for Nix in St. Louis. When I next heard of him, he was down at Chandler helping Bill Tilghman make a movie about Oklahoma outlaws.

Al Jennings had been discharged from the Ohio penitentiary on a legal technicality in 1902 and granted a full-citizenship pardon by President Theodore Roosevelt in February 1907. He had opened a law office in Oklahoma City and been defeated in his bid for prosecuting attorney of Oklahoma County in November 1912. He was again defeated as an "empty our prisons and fill them with Oklahoma's crooked politicians" candidate for governor against Judge Robert L. Williams in 1914. Meanwhile, he

Al Jennings.

Promotion sheet for Al Jennings' film *Beating Back*.

Emmett Dalton. Photo taken in California after Dalton entered
the motion picture business.

and Will Irwin, a popular writer of the period, had coauthored a weird account of the ex-bandit's life entitled *Beating Back,* which was serialized in the *Saturday Evening Post.* A motion picture of the same title had been produced by the Thanhouser Company of New York, and Jennings was touring the country with the film, lecturing on his return to respectability.

Emmett Dalton also was on the lecture circuit with a three-reeler depicting his train- and bank-robbing past, entitled *The Last Stand of the Dalton Boys.* Shot on location and including people who actually took part in the Coffeyville disaster, *Last Stand* contained a great deal of documentary material. In comparison, the Jennings five-reeler portrayed his followers as gallant cowboys who had been wronged, federal judges and district attorneys as crooks, and territorial marshals as either cold-blooded killers or sniveling cowards. Its attack on Bud Ledbetter was such that the old marshal opined he should have shot Al in the head instead of the thigh in the battle at the Spike S ranch.

Other deputy marshals, former U.S. attorneys, and judges were incensed by the lies and declared that "the present generation ought to be shown the truth." In 1915, Nix, Tilghman, and Chris Madsen formed the Eagle Film Company, their production to be the antithesis of *Beating Back,* entitled *The Passing of the Oklahoma Outlaws.* The film would deal primarily with the destruction of the Doolin and Jennings gangs—its purpose "to impress upon the young people of the country that never did the outlaw succeed and that any but an upright and law-abiding life must inevitably result in ruin."

The company's base of operations was Tilghman's Bell Cow Creek ranch northwest of Chandler. Bill's longtime friend, J.B. "Benny" Kent of Chandler, who owned a W.E. Curtis movie camera and knew much about the film art of that time, was the photographer. There was no plot. The events connected with the breaking up of the Doolin and Jennings outlaws were scripted by Capt. L.P. "Lute" Stover, a successful Kansas playwright and experienced motion picture feature director. Tilghman, Nix, Madsen, ex-Chief Deputy John Hale, U.S. attorney Caleb R. Brooks, and Arkansas Tom appeared personally in the film. Well-known performers from the Miller Brothers 101 Ranch and Pawnee Bill Wild West shows impersonated gang members. Benny Kent's wife and daughter Faye starred in female roles, and other Chandler residents served as possemen and supporting characters.

Robbery scenes were shot at nearby Merrick, against the picturesque rolling hills of Lincoln County. Otherwise, historical accuracy was achieved "where possible." The famous cave in the Creek Nation, the Dunn ranch, and Raidler's hideout in the Osage became important settings. Doolin's escape was restaged at the federal jail in Guthrie, followed by his death at Lawson. The crew traveled to Eureka Springs to enact the bandit chief's capture, and on return, filmed the Spike S ranch battle and capture of the Jennings gang on location, with Ledbetter playing himself and acting as technical adviser. In the climactic gunfight at Ingalls, Arkansas Tom played himself and provided inside information on the Doolin gang's maneuverings.

Script writer Stover saw fit to add "romantic interest" to the Ingalls fight. Wasn't Bitter Creek Newcomb the "lover" of the Wild Bunch? Why shouldn't his sweetheart rescue him after the killing of Dick Speed? Tilghman didn't like the idea, but "went along" with it. Who might this "sweetheart" be? Stover said, "We'll call her the Rose of Cimarron."

In the film, the Rose is in an upstairs room of the hotel. She sees Newcomb in the street, shot from his horse, lying helpless and bleeding badly. Anxious for his safety, she grabs up a Winchester and two belts of ammunition, slides from the window down a rope made of torn bedclothes, and carries them to her lover. But Newcomb is too weak to use the Winchester. She helps him onto his horse and mounts in front of him. With Newcomb clinging to her, both arms around her waist, the pair dash from town while stunned officers withhold their fire.

As Tilghman toured the country with *The Passing of the Oklahoma Outlaws*, lecturing his audience from the theater stage and introducing Arkansas Tom as the lone

Advertising posters for *The Passing of the Oklahoma Outlaws*.

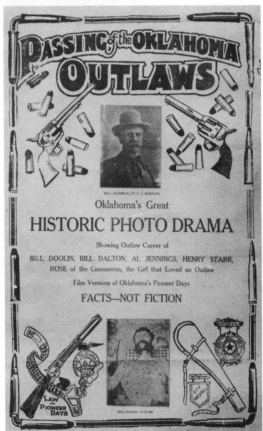

survivor of the Wild Bunch, he was asked constantly, "Who was the Rose?" Bill always replied, "Oh, just an outlaw's girl, who finally married a good man and reared a fine family. I cannot reveal her identity."

Thus began a canard that has confounded "historians" for more than half a century. After Tilghman's death in 1924, his widow, Zoe A. Tilghman (who should have known better) perpetuated Stover's concoctions, because (she told me in 1959) "Bill didn't lie" and she did not wish the public to form any "adverse opinion" of her husband. Ingalls descendants still repeat the legend and "remember" the Rose as one person or another. Apocryphal tales continue to be written by uninformed journalists. The pros and cons of the issue would fill a volume.

Contemporary reports and official records do not mention the Rose of Cimarron incident. "It didn't happen," said J.N. Fallis. "I was in and around Ingalls during the gay nineties and never heard of a character of the kind until many years later." Billy McGinty "never heard of her until Tilghman made that movie." As the Selph brothers aptly put it, "The only sweetheart Bitter Creek had in Ingalls was one of those girls at Sadie Comley's."

Appearing before unsympathetic audiences made Arkansas Tom "restless." He left the show in less than a year and returned to St. Louis, where he frequently was seen "hanging around with tough characters." In December 1916, he was arrested for a bank burglary at Neosho, Missouri. Convicted at the February term of the Newton County Circuit Court, he was sentenced to eight years in the penitentiary at Jefferson City. He was discharged from the Missouri prison in 1921 and spent the next two years in the Tri-State area around Galena.

On the afternoon of November 26, 1923, four men held up the bank at Asbury, Missouri. By the summer of 1924, two of the gang had been convicted and sent to prison, a third had been jailed on a charge of first degree robbery, and authorities were searching for Arkansas Tom. Joplin police detectives W.F. Gibson and Len Van Deventer found him August 16, hiding at the home of a friend on West Ninth Street. Tom opened fire and tried to escape. The of-

The fifteen-foot monument erected at Ingalls in memory of Deputy U.S. Marshals Dick Speed, Tom Hueston, and Lafe Shadley, who fell in the outlaw battle of September 1, 1893. The round stone at the top of the monument was taken from a well near Falls City, where outlaw wounds were dressed after the gunfight. In 1982, this monument was backed into by an oil company truck, which shattered the native sandstone and mortar structure from its base. It has not been rebuilt. The cavity in the base, sealed by the metal plaque honoring the slain marshals, contained documents and other items pertinent to Ingalls' past—to be reexamined in 1988. The cavity was vandalized and the papers and items stolen.

ficers brought him down with a bullet above the heart.

Few were left in Ingalls to mourn the death of the last of the Wild Bunch. Ingalls, too, had met its fate. During and after World War I, its remaining merchants had cast their lot with Cushing and Stillwater. Even the name itself disappeared. A reprieve seemed possible when oil was discovered in the area. The Post Office Department arbitrarily assigned the name Signet to the town in 1921. But the oil boom was short-lived. By the mid-1920s, Signet also was a village of ghosts.

Arkansas Tom Jones and the town that had made him so infamous had passed into history together.

BIBLIOGRAPHY

Manuscripts and Documents

Dalton Brothers Gang, 1891–94. Pinkerton Detective Agency file.
Eagle Film Company Tour and Account Record. Author's collection.
In re Jennings. 118 Federal Reporter 479.
In the Matter of the Application of Matthew McClaskey for a Writ of Habeas Corpus. 2 Oklahoma Reports 568.
In the Matter of the Application of William J. Raidler for a Writ of Habeas Corpus. 4 Oklahoma Reports 417.
Ingalls, Payne County, O.T. Plat and Survey adopted September 26, 1892.
Jennings vs. United States. 2 Indian Territory Reports 670.
Memorandum, Notes of the Town of Ingalls. Diary of Dr. Jacob Hiram Pickering, 1893–98.
Memorial in Death of Lafe Shadley by Citizens of Osage Reservation. Osage Agency, September 7, 1893.
Report of the Governor of Oklahoma Territory, 1892.
Report of the Secretary of the Interior for 1891. *House Executive Documents*, 52nd Cong. 1st Session, XIV.
Heck Thomas Papers. Clippings, correspondence, and marshals' records. Author's collection.
Territory of Oklahoma vs. Tom Jones. Case No. 323, District Court of Payne County, 1893–94.
Tom Jones vs. The Territory of Oklahoma. 4 Oklahoma Reports 45.

Tract Book No. 40, Ingalls, O.T. Department of the Interior, General Land Office, Washington, D.C., 1892.
Wilson, Edna Eaton. "The Story of Ingalls." Undated ms. in Stillwater Public Library.

Correspondence

Citizens' Letters. July 10–31, 1896. Department of Justice, File 12014, No. 19536.
Cooper, Frank C. To Glenn Shirley. March-April 1955.
Dale, Chief Justice Frank, First Judicial District, Territory of Oklahoma. To Richard Olney, Attorney General. May 21, 1894. Department of Justice, File 12014, No. 5955.
Fallis, J.N. To E.J. Selph. January 31 and February 22, 1955.
Fleming, Richard L. (husband of Rose Dunn). To Glenn Shirley. October 12, November 7 and 28, 1960, and February 2, 1961.
Harp, Addie C. To Bill Hoge. (Quoted in *Tulsa World*, January 23, 1955.)
Hickle, Tamie (Dunn family genealogist). To Glenn Shirley. August 31, 1982, and October 11 and 26, 1982.
Lamar, J.T., Record Clerk, Missouri State Penitentiary, Jefferson City. To Glenn Shirley. October 30, 1951.
Nagle, Patrick S. To Attorney General. August 1, 1896. Department of Justice, File 12014, No. 14620.
_____ . To Attorney General. September 14, 1896. Department of Justice, File 12014, No. 14620.
Nix, E.D. To Attorney General Olney. January 16, 1894. Department of Justice, File 12014, No. 687.
_____ . (By Chief Deputy Hale.) To Maj. Frank Strong, General Agent, U.S. Department of Justice. January 31, 1894. Department of Justice, File 12014.
_____ . Telegram to Attorney General Olney. February 15, 1894. U.S. Department of Justice, File 1951.
_____ . To Attorney General Olney, March 20, 1894. Records of United States Marshal for Oklahoma Territory, Guthrie, 1893–94, Department of Justice, File 12014.
_____ . To Attorney General. September 5, 1894. Department of Justice, File 12014, No. 10297.
_____ . To Attorney General. May 3 and 14, 1895. Department of Justice, File 7114.
_____ . To Attorney General Olney. July 30, 1895. Records of United States Marshal for Oklahoma Territory, Guthrie, 1893–95.

Norris, Dwane V. (Shadley family genealogist). To Glenn Shirley. August 21, 1989.

Selph, Ernest J. To Joe Austell Small. August 23, 1954.

Shadley, Miles A. III. To Glenn Shirley. September 1, 1977.

Thomas, Albert M. To Glenn Shirley. October 7, 1957.

U.S. Attorney Brooks. To Attorney General Judson Harmon. April 11, 1896. Records of District Attorney for Oklahoma Territory, Guthrie, 1896.

_____ . To Attorney General Judson Harmon. October 14, 1896. Records of District Attorney, Guthrie, O.T., October 1896.

U.S. Attorney. To Attorney General Joseph McKenna. December 3, 1897. Records of District Attorney, Guthrie, O.T., December 1897.

Wilson, C.W., Record Clerk, Kansas State Penitentiary, Lansing. To Glenn Shirley. November 1, 1951.

Interviews

Catelou, Jennie Watt. *Indian-Pioneer History, Foreman Collection.* Vol. 77. Oklahoma Historical Society.

Lucas, Orrington. *Indian-Pioneer History, Foreman Collection.* Vol. 61. Oklahoma Historical Society.

McGinty, Billy. Personal interviews. 1957–58.

Pickering, Earl and LeRoy "Roy." Personal interviews. 1957–58.

Selph, Ernest and Harry. Personal interviews. 1954–55.

Sollers, O.W. Personal interview. June 1940.

Thompson, H.A. "Hi." Personal interview. June 1940.

Wagner, Walter. Personal interview. 1955.

Williams, Jim. *Indian-Pioneer History, Foreman Collection.* Vol. 49. Oklahoma Historical Society.

Newspapers

Afton (Oklahoma) *Herald.* May 1894.

Arapaho (Oklahoma) *Argus.* March 1896.

Chandler (Oklahoma) *News–Publicist.* January, February, May 1915.

Cherokee Advocate (Tahlequah, Oklahoma). September 1893; May 1894.

Coffeyville (Kansas) *Journal.* October, November 1892.

Cushing (Oklahoma) *Daily Citizen.* October 1934.

Cushing (Oklahoma) *Herald.* November 1897.

Daily Oklahoman (Oklahoma City). June 1894; September,

December 1895; July 1896; June 1904; August 1952; October 1989.

Dodge City (Kansas) *Globe.* November, December 1892.

El Reno (Oklahoma) *Democrat.* April 1894.

El Reno (Oklahoma) *Globe.* April 1895.

El Reno (Oklahoma) *News.* July 1896.

Enid (Oklahoma) *Daily Wave.* April 1895.

Fort Smith (Arkansas) *Elevator.* May, September 1891; June 1892; September 1895.

Guthrie (Oklahoma) *Daily Leader.* September, December 1893; May, June, October 1894; April, May, September 1895; January, May, June, July, August 1896; November, December 1897; April 1898.

Guthrie (Oklahoma) *Daily News.* June 1893.

Hennessey (Oklahoma) *Clipper.* April 1895.

Joplin (Missouri) *Globe.* August 1924.

Kansas City (Missouri) *Times.* November 1893; March 1894.

Kingfisher (Oklahoma) *Free Press.* April 1895; April 1896.

Muskogee (Oklahoma) *Phoenix.* November 1897; February 1898; January 1915.

Norman (Oklahoma) *Transcript.* September 1891.

Oklahoma City Press-Gazette. September, October 1893.

Oklahoma City Times-Journal. August 1891.

Oklahoma Daily Press-Gazette (Oklahoma City). January, March, May, June 1894.

Oklahoma Daily Times-Journal (Oklahoma City). May, September 1895; January, March, April, May, July 1896.

Oklahoma Daily Star (Oklahoma City). April 1895.

Oklahoma Hawk (Stillwater). March 1893.

Oklahoma State Capital (Guthrie, Oklahoma). May, June, July, September, October, November 1893; January, February, March, April, May, June, October, December 1894; April, May, September 1895; January, March, April, July, August, October, December 1896; November, December 1897; April 1898; November, December 1902; November 1903; February 1905; July 1906; March, April 1908; March, August, November, December 1910.

Oklahoma State Sentinel (Stillwater). May 1894; February 1895.

Parsons (Kansas) *Daily Sun.* July 1892.

Pawnee (Oklahoma) *Scout.* January 1894.

Pawnee (Oklahoma) *Times.* January 1894.

Pawnee (Oklahoma) *Times-Democrat.* May 1895.

Perkins (Oklahoma) *Journal.* September 1893.

The Populist (Stillwater, Oklahoma). October 1895.

Star and Kansan (Independence, Kansas). September 1893.

Ripley (Oklahoma) *Review*. September 1941.

Stillwater (Oklahoma) *Advance*. June, July 1904.

Stillwater (Oklahoma) *Eagle-Gazette*. January, February, March, May, June, July, August, December 1894.

Stillwater (Oklahoma) *Gazette*. July, October, November, December 1892; June, July, September, December 1893; June 1894; October, November 1895; May, September, December 1896; April, October 1901; February, June, July 1902; May, June 1903; June 1904; February, May, June 1905; July, August, September 1906; March, April 1908.

Stillwater (Oklahoma) *News-Press*. November 1953; February, May 1954; April 1989.

Tulsa (Oklahoma) *World*. March 1955.

Vinita (Oklahoma) *Indian Chieftain*. February, September 1890; September, October 1891; July, November 1892.

Vinita (Oklahoma) *Leader*. September 1895.

Books and Pamphlets

Block, Eugene B. *Great Train Robberies of the West*. New York: Coward-McCann, 1959.

Canton, Frank M. *Frontier Trails*. Boston: Houghton Mifflin Company, 1930.

Chapman, Berlin Basil. *The Founding of Stillwater*. Oklahoma City: Times Journal Publishing Company, 1948.

Croy, Homer. *Trigger Marshal: The Story of Chris Madsen*. New York: Duell, Sloan and Pearce, 1958.

Cunningham, Robert E. *Stillwater, Where Oklahoma Began*. Stillwater: Arts and Humanities Council, 1969.

Dalton, Emmett. *When the Daltons Rode*. New York: Doubleday, Doran and Company, 1931.

Dillon, Richard. *Wells, Fargo Detective: The Biography of James B. Hume*. New York: Coward-McCann, 1969.

Drago, Harry Sinclair. *Outlaws on Horseback*. New York: Dodd, Mead and Company, 1964.

Elliott, David Stewart. *Last Raid of the Daltons, A Reliable Recital of the Battle With the Bandits at Coffeyville, Kansas, October 5, 1892*. Coffeyville, Kansas. Coffeyville Daily Journal, 1892.

"An Eye Witness." *The Dalton Brothers and Their Astounding Career of Crime*. Chicago: Laird and Lee, 1892.

Foreman, Carolyn Thomas. *Oklahoma Imprints 1835–1907: A History of Printing in Oklahoma Before Statehood.* Norman: University of Oklahoma Press, 1936.

Gittinger, Roy. *The Formation of the State of Oklahoma, 1803–1906.* Berkeley: University of California Press, 1917.

Glasscock, C.B. *Bandits and the Southern Pacific.* New York: Frederick A. Stokes Company, 1929.

Graves, Richard S. *Oklahoma Outlaws.* Oklahoma City: State Printing and Publishing Company, 1915.

Halsell, H.H. *Cowboys and Cattleland.* Nashville: The Parthenon Press, 1937.

Hanes, Bailey. *Bill Doolin, Outlaw, O.T.* Norman: University of Oklahoma Press, 1968.

Harman, S.W. *Hell on the Border: He Hanged Eighty-Eight Men.* Fort Smith, Arkansas: Phoenix Publishing Company, 1898.

History of Custer and Washita Counties. Clinton, Oklahoma: Clinton Daily News, 1937.

Horan, James D. *The Authentic Wild West—The Lawmen.* New York: Crown Publishers, Inc., 1980.

_____ . *Desperate Men, Revelations From the Sealed Pinkerton Files.* New York: G.P. Putnam's Sons, 1949.

_____ . *Desperate Women.* New York: G.P. Putnam's Sons, 1952.

Hutchinson, W.H. *A Bar Cross Man.* Norman: University of Oklahoma Press, 1956.

Jennings, Al. With Will Irwin. *Beating Back.* New York: D. Appleton and Company, 1914.

Jones, William F. *The Experience of A Deputy U.S. Marshal of the Indian Territory.* Privately printed, 1937.

Lake, Carolyn, ed. *Under Cover For Wells Fargo: The Unvarnished Recollections of Fred Dodge.* Boston: Houghton Mifflin Company, 1969.

Latta, Frank F. *Dalton Gang Days.* Santa Cruz, California: Bear State Books, 1976.

McNeal, T.A. *When Kansas Was Young.* New York: MacMillan Company, 1922.

Morgan, Jonnie R. *The History of Wichita Falls.* Wichita Falls: Nortex Offset Publications, 1971.

Newsom, J.A. *The Life and Practice of the Wild and Modern Indian, The Early Days of Oklahoma.* Oklahoma City: Harlow Publishing Company, 1923.

Nix, Evett Dumas. *Oklahombres, Particularly the Wilder Ones.* St. Louis: Eden Publishing Company, 1929.

Paine, Albert Bigelow. *Captain Bill McDonald, Texas Ranger.*

New York: J.J. Little and Ives Company, 1909.

Rainey, George. *The Cherokee Strip*. Guthrie, Oklahoma: Co-Operative Publishing Company, 1933.

_____ . *No Man's Land: The Historic Story of a Landed Orphan*. Guthrie, Oklahoma: Co-Operative Publishing Company, 1937.

Rhodes, May Davison. *The Hired Man on Horseback*. Boston: Houghton Mifflin Company, 1938.

Ridings, Sam P. *The Chisholm Trail*. Guthrie, Oklahoma: Co-Operative Publishing Company, 1936.

Samuelson, Nancy B. *The Dalton Gang Family, A Genealogical Study of the Dalton Outlaws and Their Family Connections*. Privately printed, 1989.

Shirk, George H. *Oklahoma Place Names*. Norman: University of Oklahoma Press, 1965.

Shirley, Glenn. *Guardian of the Law: The Life and Times of William Matthew Tilghman, 1854-1924*. Austin, Texas: Eakin Press, 1988.

_____ . *Heck Thomas, Frontier Marshal: The Story of a Real Gunfighter*. Philadelphia: Chilton Company, 1962. New edition, Norman: University of Oklahoma Press, 1981.

_____ . *West of Hell's Fringe: Crime, Criminals and the Federal Peace Officer in Oklahoma Territory, 1889-1907*. Norman: University of Oklahoma Press, 1978.

Stansbery, Lon R. *The Passing of the 3-D Ranch*. Tulsa, Oklahoma: George Henry Printing Company, n.d.

Starr, Helen, and O.E. Hill. *Footprints in the Indian Nation*. Muskogee, Oklahoma: Hoffman Printing Company, 1974.

Stewart, Dora Ann. *The Government and Development of Oklahoma Territory*. Oklahoma City: Harlow Publishing Company, 1933.

Sullivan, W.J.L. *Twelve Years in the Saddle for Law and Order on the Frontiers of Texas*. Austin: Von Boeckmann-Jones Company, 1909.

Sutton, Fred E. As told to A.B. McDonald. *Hands Up! Stories of the Six-Gun Fighters of the Old Wild West*. Indianapolis: Bobbs-Merrill Company, 1927.

Tilghman, Zoe A. *Outlaw Days*. Oklahoma City: Harlow Publishing Company, 1926.

Wellman, Paul I. *A Dynasty of Western Outlaws*. New York: Doubleday and Company, Inc., 1961.

Wells, Laura Lou. *Young Cushing in Oklahoma Territory*. Stillwater, Oklahoma: Frontier Printers, Inc., n.d.

Wood, Sylvan R., and Preston George. *The Railroads of Oklahoma*. Boston: The Railway and Locomotive Historical Society, Inc., Baker Library, Harvard Business School, 1943.

Wright, Muriel H., and Joseph B. Thoburn. *Oklahoma: A History of the State and Its People*. New York: Lewis Historical Publishing Company, 1929. Vol. II.

Articles

Burchardt, Bill. "Trail and Furrow." *Oklahoma Today*, Spring 1971.

Castleman, Sean. "Arkansas Tom, Last of the Horseback Outlaws." *Oldtimers Wild West*, August 1979.

Chapman, Basil Berlin. "Ingalls Reunion Recalls History." *Stillwater News-Press*, September 5, 1965.

"Cimarron Rose Legend Dies—Husband Tells True Story." *Daily Oklahoman*, October 2, 1955.

Cooper, Frank C. "Santa Fe Passenger Train Holdups in Oklahoma During the '90's." *Santa Fe Magazine*, April 1955.

Cortesi, Lawrence. "The Bloody Shootout at Murray's Saloon." *Frontier West*, August 1972.

Cunningham, Robert E. "Ghost Towns Mark Payne County." *Stillwater News-Press*, August 28, 1967.

_____ . "Ingalls Was Given Bad Reputation That Eventually Wiped Out Town." *Stillwater News-Press*, June 24, 1963.

_____ . "They Ran Again in '91." *Oklahoma's Orbit*, September 17, 1961.

Dalton, Emmett. "Beyond the Law." *Wide World Magazine*, May-September 1918.

Dellinger, Doris. "Former Ingalls Hotel, Hester Street House Touch of History." *Stillwater News-Press*, February 17, 1982.

Dunn, Warren. "Bob Andrews, Fearless As Pioneer Lawman." *Stillwater News-Press*, March 10, 1954.

"Early Territory Outlaw Haven." *Guthrie Daily Leader*, '89er Edition, April 1983.

Franklin, Tena. "Early Years of '89ers Told; First on Agenda Was House." *Stillwater News-Press*, April 18, 1954.

"From Prosecuted to Prosecutor." *Literary Digest*, September 21, 1912.

Gage, Duane. "Al Jennings: The People's Choice." *Chronicles of Oklahoma*, Vol. XLVI, No. 3, Autumn 1968.

Garrett, Mrs. Frank. "Jesse Denton Ramsey." *Chronicles of*

Comanche County (Oklahoma), Vol. II, No. 1, Spring 1956.

Gibbs, Lawrence. "Stillwater Hasn't Always Been Derailed." *Stillwater News-Press*, April 21, 1976.

Glynn, Dean. "The Last Fight of the Wild Bunch." *Westerner*, July-August 1970.

Harmon, Bill. "Old Timer Has Own Ideas About Handling Repeal." *Stillwater News-Press*, December 7, 1958.

_____. "Outlaws Keep Peace at Bar." *Daily Oklahoman*, December 7, 1958.

Hauton, Bob and Catherine. "Ingalls—Old Lawman-Bandit Battleground No Ghost Town." *Daily Oklahoman*, July 12, 1970.

"Hotel-Turned-House Holds History of Fight." *Stillwater Star*, March 10, 1960.

Human, Wayne. "Excitement Ran High in 1902 When 'Iron Horse' Appeared in Stillwater." *Stillwater News-Press*, November 24, 1970.

"Ingalls' Historic 'Bloody 1893' Related by Old-Timer Who Saw it All." *Payne County News*, October 19, 1928.

"Ingalls, Okla. Boomed From Beginning." *Stillwater News-Press*, July 13, 1983.

Ingram, John E. "Ingalls, Oklahoma Territory." *Oklahoma Ranch and Farm World*, August 9, 1959.

Ironsides, R.P. "Desperate Battle with Outlaws." *Frontier Times*, September 1951.

James, Carey. "The Mystery of Cimarron Rose." *Zane Grey Western Magazine*, August 1971.

Kerr, William Ray. "In Defense of Ingalls, Oklahoma." *True West*, September-October 1964.

King, Sterling Price. As told to Frederick E. Voelker. "More Rose of Cimarron." *True West*, May-June 1955.

Koller, Joe. "Bloody Ingalls Under Siege." *The West*, December 1967.

"Living Witness of Famous Ingalls Gun Battle." *Tel-ectric Topics* (Kingfisher, Oklahoma), December 1973.

McRill, Leslie. "Old Ingalls: The Story of a Town That Will Not Die." *Chronicles of Oklahoma*, Vol. XXVI, No. 4, Winter 1958–59.

Nelson, Dan. "The Ingalls Raid." *Daily O'Collegian* (Stillwater, Oklahoma), Literary Supplement, May 2, 1926.

"Old Hotel Has Exciting History." *Oklahoma's Orbit*, October 22, 1961.

Oldham, Maggie Rex. "Rose of Cimarron." *True West*, August-

September 1954.

Peterson, Elmer R. "A Ghost Comes to Life." *Daily Oklahoman*, September 11, 1938.

"Power of Outlaw Bill Doolin Gang Ended With Blazing Gun Battle 60 Years Ago at Ingalls." *Perry Daily Journal*, September 14, 1953.

Powers, Mark. "The Doolin Gang's Last Shoot-Out." *True Frontier*, Special Issue No. 1, "Best of the Bad Men," 1971.

Rickards, Colin. "Last of the Horseback Outlaws." *Frontier Times*, April-May 1971.

Rouse, M.C. "Pleasant Valley and Cowboy Flat." *True West*, July-August 1968.

"The Rush to Oklahoma." *Harper's Weekly*, October 3, 1891.

Shirk, George H. "First Post Offices Within the Boundaries of Oklahoma." *Chronicles of Oklahoma*, Vol. XXVI, No. 2, Summer 1948, and Vol. XXX, No. 1, Spring 1952.

Shirley, Glenn. "Death of 'Terrible' Bill Doolin." *Modern Man*, January 1959.

_____. "The Rose of Cimarron Myth." *True West*, August-September 1954.

Shoemaker, Elsie. "Oldtimers Recall Ingalls, September 1, 1893." *Stillwater News-Press*, September 6, 1964.

Stansbery, Lon R. " 'Cops and Robbers' of Territorial Days." *Tulsa Daily World*, December 20, 1936.

Stiles, George W. "Early Days in the Sac and Fox Country, Oklahoma Territory." *Chronicles of Oklahoma*, Vol. XXXIII, No. 3, Autumn 1955.

Swett, Morris. "Al J. Jennings." *Chronicles of Comanche County* (Oklahoma), Vol. VI, No. 2, Autumn 1960.

Tilghman, Zoe A. "I Knew Rose of the Cimarron." *True West*, May-June 1958.

Turner, Elaine. "Davis Family Eye-Witness to Ingalls' History." *Mannford Eagle*, September 10, 1981.

Walker, Wayne T. "Arkansas Tom, Gunslinger." *Great West*, December 1973. Reprinted in *Authentic West*, Spring 1981.

_____. "Jim Masterson, The Loner." *Great West*, August 1971.

_____. "Jim Masterson, Quiet Marshal." *Real West Yearbook*, Summer 1978.

Wallace, John. "The Story of a U.S. Marshal, Red Lucas." *Frontier Times*, June-July 1974.

Wilkerson, Ron. "3 Deputies Die in Clash With Outlaws, 77 Years Ago Ingalls Exploded in Gun Battle." *Stillwater News-Press*, October 6, 1970.

Wilson, Edna Eaton. "When the Blood Spilled in County Gun-fight in 1893." *Stillwater News-Press*, March 2, 1960.

INDEX

INGALLS, O.T.
1893

MAIN STREET

STILLWATER
WAGON

LUCAS
SURVEY
OUTFIT

WALNUT STREET

THIRD S

N
W E
S

LEGEND

1. Light, Blacksmith
2. Sanders' Barber Shop
3. Ketchum's Boot Shop
4. Briggs' Office
5. Wagner's Blacksmith
6. Sadie Comley
7. Call's Residence
8. Selph Grocery
9. Wagner Home
10. Dr. Selph's Office
11. Dr. Call's Office and Pharmacy
12. McMurtry's Drugstore/Undertaker
    Gully